Jay P. Granat, PhD

Persuasive Advertising for Entrepreneurs and Small Business Owners: How to Create More Effective Sales Messages

Persuasive Advertising for Entrepreneurs and Small Business Owners

How to Create More Effective Sales Messages

HAWORTH Marketing Resources:
Innovations in Practice & Professional Services
William J. Winston, Senior Editor

New, Recent, and Forthcoming Titles:

Long Term Care Administration: The Management of Institutional and Non-Institutional Components of the Continuum of Care by Ben Abramovice

Cases and Select Readings in Health Care Marketing edited by Robert E. Sweeney, Robert L. Berl, and William J. Winston

Marketing Planning Guide by Robert E. Stevens, David L. Loudon, and William E. Warren

Marketing for Churches and Ministries by Robert E. Stevens and David L. Loudon

The Clinician's Guide to Managed Mental Health Care by Norman Winegar

A Guide to Preparing Cost-Effective Press Releases by Robert H. Loeffler

How to Create Interest-Evoking, Sales-Inducing, Non-Irritating Advertising by Walter Weir

Professional Services Marketing: Strategy and Tactics by F. G. Crane

Market Analysis: Assessing Your Business Opportunities by Robert E. Stevens, Philip K. Sherwood, and J. Paul Dunn

Marketing for Attorneys and Law Firms edited by William J. Winston

Selling Without Confrontation by Jack Greening

Persuasive Advertising for Entrepreneurs and Small Business Owners: How to Create More Effective Sales Messages by Jay P. Granat

Marketing Mental Health Services in a Managed Care Environment by Norman Winegar and John L. Bistline

Persuasive Advertising for Entrepreneurs and Small Business Owners
How to Create More Effective Sales Messages

Jay P. Granat, PhD

The Haworth Press
New York • London • Norwood (Australia)

The Haworth Press, Inc., 10 Alice Street, Binghamton, NY 13904-1580

Paperback edition published in 1997.

Library of Congress Cataloging-in-Publication Data

Granat, Jay P.
  Persuasive advertising for entrepreneurs and small business owners: how to create more effective sales messages / Jay P. Granat.
      p.   cm.
  Includes bibliographical references (p.) and index.
  ISBN 1-56024-994-3 (acid-free paper).
  1. Advertising–Psychological aspects. 2. Persuasion (Psychology) 3. Small business–Marketing. I. Title
HF5822.G7 1993
659.1–dc20   92-22807
                                                                            CIP

To my beautiful wife, Robin, who has always shown never-ending
support for my entrepreneurial spirit.

And to all those who have ever had the
courage and tenacity to work for themselves.

ABOUT THE AUTHOR

Jay P. Granat, PhD, has developed successful advertisements, television and radio commercials, direct mail programs, and public relations campaigns for a wide range of products and services. A trained psychotherapist, he is particularly interested in the psychological factors that impact on and influence consumer behavior. Dr. Granat has written many articles on advertising, marketing, and public relations and has lectured extensively on entrepreneurship and business development. The winner of an advertising award from The Ad Club of New York, he established a phone consultation hotline to assist entrepreneurs with their advertising and business problems. If you have any questions about your company's advertising or about building your business, you can call him at (201) 592-6420, fax him at (201) 363-0859, or write to him at The Skyline Consultation Group, 2015 Center Ave., 2nd Floor, Fort Lee, N.J. 07024.

CONTENTS

The Power of Persuasive Advertising

One direct response newspaper advertisement has made hundreds of thousands of dollars for a publishing company.

Many large businesses have been built with small classified advertisements.

One entrepreneur makes seventeen dollars for every dollar he spends on advertising in the yellow pages.

Increasingly, companies are relying on advertising that produces quantifiable results.

Many advertisements generate three hundred percent return.

Direct response radio and television commercials can cause your phone to ring immediately.

Persuasive advertising can build an image and increase sales simultaneously.

An Inspirational Message
for Entrepreneurs

The credit belongs to the man
who is actually in the arena,
who strives valiantly . . .
who knows the great
enthusiasms,
the great devotions . . .
and spends himself
in a worthy cause,
who at the best,
knows the triumph
of high achievement;
and who at the worst,
if he fails . . . at least he fails
while daring greatly,
so that his place shall never
be with cold and timid souls
who know neither
victory nor defeat.

Theodore Roosevelt

Author's Note

Due to production limitations, some advertisements and brochures could not be included in this book. If you would like to obtain copies of these materials, they can be obtained by contacting the author.

Chapter 1

Introduction

WHAT WILL ENTREPRENEURS LEARN FROM THIS BOOK?

- You will learn how to think like an advertising professional and be able to distinguish potentially successful advertisements from potentially unsuccessful ones. This will help you make more money with your advertising and save more money on your advertising.

- You will develop the skills that you need to create effective advertisements and commercials.

- You will find out how hypnosis and hypnotic principles can help you to increase the effectiveness of your sales messages.

- You will learn how to select the appropriate media for your sales messages.

- You will discover how to use public relations in conjunction with your advertising.

- You will see examples of successful and unsuccessful campaigns.

- You will learn how to work more effectively with advertising agencies and advertising consultants.

WHO SHOULD READ THIS BOOK?

The information in this book should be of interest to entrepreneurs, small business owners, copywriters, chief executive officers, product managers, brand managers, advertising educators, and marketing directors.

In short, this book should be of interest to anyone who is concerned with creating more effective and more persuasive sales messages.

WHAT'S DIFFERENT ABOUT THIS BOOK?

Most advertising books for small business owners follow a rather uniform pattern. They begin with a brief overview of advertising and marketing, define some key terms, review some guidelines and formulas for creating good advertisements and commercials, and then show samples of effective campaigns. To be honest, when I initially thought about writing this book, I planned on creating a manual that followed the same general outline.

Fortunately, a few months after signing my contract with The Haworth Press, I had a brief but exceedingly valuable phone conversation with William Winston, my editor. Bill suggested that I include a lot of my personal experiences in the book. He felt this would make the book more interesting and would help me to teach the advertising concepts in a more innovative and proficient manner. I believe Bill is right.

In addition, if I evaluate myself as if I were a product and ask myself, What sets me apart from others who have written on advertising? I would have to say that it is probably the fact that I have a rather unique background compared with other people who work in this business.

As is noted in the "About The Author" section, I have had a diverse array of experiences. I have run a publishing company as well as an advertising agency. I am also a college professor and a psychotherapist. I have won advertising awards and have been a judge in advertising contests. I have been fortunate enough to create campaigns for a wide range of products and services.

My clients have included health care facilities, law firms, pharmaceutical companies, dentists, construction companies, photographers, software companies, video production companies, caterers, accounting firms, graphic artists, printers, psychologists, weight control clinics, accounting firms, drug treatment facilities, inventors, and consultants. I have also written ads and commercials for books, video and audio cassette programs, and seminars.

I believe that all of these business and life experiences make it possible for me to provide other entrepreneurs and would-be entrepreneurs with some rather novel insights into the ad game. I hope that my broad range of life experiences will allow me to impart some useful information to you. Again, I believe Bill Winston is right and that a book that includes a personal tone will be more interesting and instructive than a book outlining theories, lists, rules, and guidelines.

I have given dozens of seminars on advertising, marketing, and public relations to a wide range of audiences, and I have noted that invariably workshop participants are very interested in the instructor's background and experiences. While I am not one to spend a lot of time recalling advertising war stories when teaching my college courses and workshops, I have observed that students listen very closely when I integrate a campaign that I have worked on into one of my lectures.

Moreover, many students are far more interested in real-life experiences than they are in the theoretical kind of information contained in most textbooks. As I mulled over Bill's advice, it occurred to me that a personalized book would probably be more fun to write–and hopefully more fun to read–than would a straightforward manual that resembles a textbook for small business people and entrepreneurs.

Throughout this book, I will integrate anecdotes about my advertising and business successes and failures. I will also try to tell you as many relevant tales as are needed in order to clarify and enliven the concepts under discussion.

ONE ENTREPRENEUR TO ANOTHER

Entrepreneurs are a rather special breed. Like a lot of you who are reading this book, I am an entrepreneur who has both made a lot of money and wasted a lot of money on all forms of promotion. I know what it is like to try to make decisions about copy, media, and advertising budgets.

Moreover, I have a gut-level understanding of the stress, anxiety, and challenges that entrepreneurs encounter on a daily basis. I know what it's like to stay up all night worrying about a big loan or a big cash investment in a venture. I also know what it's like to have a burning desire to see a creative business idea come to fruition.

I understand the powerful drive that so many people have to work for themselves. For some, self-employment is a question of getting away from a difficult boss. Others want the freedom and independence that their own business provides. Some entrepreneurs lack the tolerance and patience for corporate meetings and for large, cumbersome bureaucracies that move at a snail's pace. My wife, who has just started her own psychotherapy practice, and who has been bitten by the entrepreneurial bug, recently told me, "I don't know how I ever put up with traveling into Manhattan every day. Besides, I'm really glad to be away from that pain-in-the-ass boss of mine."

Other entrepreneurs catch the fever by watching a parent or loved one build a family business. When these youngsters enter the world of work, they often feel destined to have their own venture. Some simply want to model the behavior of an adult role model. Others are quite competitive where parents and significant role models are concerned, and they are compulsively driven to outdo and surpass what their parents have accomplished.

The point I am trying to make is that I am an entrepreneur as well as an ad man. I have a lot of friends, clients, and associates who are in business for themselves. I have been in several businesses the last twelve years. I hope I will be able to relate to you in a personalized and meaningful manner because I have probably experienced many of the same thoughts, feelings, problems, and situations you have faced or are confronting right now.

In addition, because I am trained as a psychotherapist, I understand many of the conscious and unconscious emotional and motivational issues that influence advertising, sales, and human nature. As you probably know, and as you will see through the course of this book, there is great deal of psychology involved in advertising. One of the links between my training in psychology and my work in the advertising business is my interest in the roles that hypnotic techniques play in selling. Some of you may be starting to conjure up images of subliminal advertising and you may be thinking I am some kind of nut. In fact, some of my colleagues in academia looked at me as if I were a little weird when I mentioned my interest in hypnotic advertising.

Despite the fact that some of my own and others' ideas about hypnotic advertising have not yet been scientifically proven, I strongly believe there is much that entrepreneurial advertisers can learn by viewing advertising as being similar to the hypnotic process.

Also, I have been fortunate enough to do a lot of direct response advertising, which is often the kind of marketing communication the entrepreneur relies on. Many of the advertisements and commercials I have created are intended to get the phone ringing, get the checks in the mail, or get people into a store or facility. In fact, it is this kind of advertising, as opposed to image advertising, that many small businesses use most often. While some of these advertisements have enhanced a company's image over the long haul, their prime function in most cases was to get feedback in the form of sales or inquiries. In my view, direct response is the most challenging, scientific, and pragmatic form of advertising. You can actually quantify the cost-effectiveness of every dollar spent on a direct response campaign. In addition, direct response advertising and marketing are among the most powerful business tools for entrepreneurs whose companies are growing.

In addition, as many of you know, complex and multifaceted business problems and advertising problems often require multidisciplinary solutions. In other words, it is sometimes useful to be able to evaluate situations from several different perspectives. I believe my diverse background allows me to develop an overall perspective on many entrepreneurial dilemmas.

Similarly, it is quite common to find people who have diverse backgrounds within the fields of advertising, marketing, and public relations. I know a number of outstanding account executives who have backgrounds in law, accounting, and economics. Likewise, many fine copywriters have training in English, psychology, political science, or journalism. H. Gordon Lewis, a fine direct response copywriter, has written screenplays for movies. David Ogilvy, the famous ad man, had a lot of different jobs before getting into the advertising business.

Advertising is clearly an industry in which people's personal experiences play a powerful role in the business decisions they make. For instance, it is quite common for a creative director to base an advertisement or a commercial on something he or she has observed or on a memorable life experience that has been stored in the person's unconscious mind.

Like a lot of people who are drawn to the communications fields, I am an idea person. I hope that my experiences and creative juices make this book worthwhile for you. I also hope I am able to impart useful information that will show you how to produce outstanding advertising for your entrepreneurial ventures.

Chapter 2

"The Medium Is the Message"– Even for a Five-Year-Old

MY START
IN THE ADVERTISING BUSINESS

Like a lot of you who are reading this book, I grew up being fascinated by the Gillette *Friday Night Fights, Howdy Doody, Lassie, Rin Tin Tin, The Untouchables, Dragnet*, and *Leave It to Beaver*. I can also vividly recall President Kennedy's assassination, Nixon's resignation, and dramatic footage of the Vietnam War. Much to my mother's dismay, I could spend hours in front of the television feeling as intrigued by the commercials as I was by the programming. I also recall the intense excitement around my house when my father was a guest on *The Dave Garroway Show*. I sat in awe with my eyes fixed on the screen while my dad spoke about one of his business ventures.

However, my preoccupation with the electronic media was not restricted to television. . . . I can remember sneaking my transistor radio into my bed so that I could listen to the Floyd Patterson-Ingemar Johansson fight. I remember Muhammad Ali's controversial knockout of Sonny Liston as if it were yesterday. Likewise, I can still recall Mel Allen's unique voice, along with his vivid and animated descriptions of the action at the New York Yankees games: "That ball is going, going, gone. It's another long home run for Mickey Mantle."

As long as I can remember, I have been enamored with all forms of communication: radio, television, books, and magazines. As a kid, when I got interested in something, I had to read everything I could get my hands on. When I got my first dog, I read dozens of books on dog training and animal psychology. When I got into surf casting, I had to learn all I could about this form of ocean fishing. I read every magazine, book, and catalog that dealt with striped bass fishing and bluefish fishing in the Northeast. I guess I was a communications junkie at an early age. And it seems that some things never change, since I am now in the midst of a passionate love affair with Prodigy, the computer on-line system. In fact, when I take breaks from writing this book, I sign on to Prodigy to keep track of my investments, make travel plans, select restaurants, and monitor the news.

When I ask college students how advertising has affected their lives, they often have difficulty answering. Perhaps they are unaware of the impact that the thousands of messages they have been exposed to have had on their attitudes, beliefs, and feelings. Maybe they are embarrassed to admit that they have been affected by some of the nonsensical stuff that appears on the airwaves and in other media.

I, on the other hand, can vividly recall the numerous ways in which advertising and the media have influenced my life. I used to place my ear next to my bowl of Rice Krispies so I could hear the snap, crackle, and pop loud and clear. When I grew tired of this, I used to stare at the picture of Tony the Tiger on my box of Frosted Flakes. I was probably hoping he would begin to talk to me the way he did on the television commercials. I was also a real sucker for sales promotions and would try any cereal that offered a free prize. You name it: Cocoa Crispies, Sugar Pops, or Corn Flakes. Throw in a five-cent statue, game, or toy and I was sold.

I even entered contests for products I didn't use. Once, I entered a contest sponsored by Salem cigarettes. The first prize was a car. The second prize was a trip for two to Hawaii. I was only five, had no driver's license, and was single, but I was still sure I would win. And once my name was pulled out of the hat, I knew I would find some use for the prizes. As a last resort, I could always give them to my parents. It probably would have been a good idea to give them some sort of present. After all, they were quite perturbed with me for the inappropriate behavior I had engaged in while watching television a few months before entering the Salem contest.

While watching *Romper Room* one day, I made the big mistake of drawing with a crayon on the television screen. As some of you may remember, *Romper Room* viewers would be referred to as a "do bee" for good behavior and a "don't bee" if you engaged in bad behavior. One sure way to be labeled a "don't bee" was to write on the television screen without using the special plastic cover that the *Romper Room* staff would sell to young bees around the country. Despite the fact that the *Romper Room* people warned me not to use a crayon on my family's TV, I failed to listen. I wasn't really a bad kid, though. It was more that I was totally captivated by the show and so eager to participate in the class activities that I could not wait for the plastic television cover to come in the mail.

Since I mentioned the mail, I might as well tell you a little about my early experiences with this form of advertising. As was the case with television and radio advertising, my introduction to the world of mail order, direct response advertising, and mail order marketing also began at age five. This time I responded to another important advertising medium for children–comic books.

The back of one of my *Superman* comics contained an advertisement for a log cabin. The picture was really enticing. There was a little boy, one of my peers, with a Davey Crockett hat and a rifle. He was having a grand old time playing just outside his log cabin. Now, I already had a clubhouse that my friends and I would spend hours in every day. But I thought a log cabin would really be terrific. Every kid on the block would want to play at my house and be my friend if I had one of these. In addition, I would be able to periodically hide from the real enemy, my parents, by secluding myself in my new log cabin. I begged my parents to give me the money to send away for this item. I believe it sold for three or four dollars. The bad part about this purchase was that I had to wait four to six weeks for the cabin to arrive. Anything more than five minutes seems like an eternity for a young child.

In spite of the fact that I had almost ruined our only television set a few weeks earlier, my parents agreed to buy me the log cabin. I waited for the mailman every day. Finally, the log cabin arrived. I was a bit perplexed when the package arrived, because it was only about the size of a loose-leaf binder. As I opened it, I was trauma-tized to discover that the log cabin was really a large plastic bag with brown logs drawn on it and dotted lines that you were sup-posed to cut out to create the windows. The package also included a few sticks designed to anchor the plastic bag. My family still makes fun of me today for making this purchase. I had had visions of a small, wooden ranch house and was devastated when I received something that looked like a grocery bag.

You would think that I would have learned my lesson about mail order buying after this experience. No way. A few months later, I noticed an advertisement on the back of one of my *Batman* comics. This one promised all kinds of "super" items: bicycles, radios, cameras, and baseball gloves. All for just a few bucks. The offer and the picture seemed so great, there was no reason for me to bother reading the small print. This time I didn't even consult my parents. With my sister's help, I sent a few bucks away so I could find out how to get these "super" prizes. I felt I could trust my sister. After all, she was seven at the time and a far more experi-enced consumer than myself. A few weeks later, I received a large tube in the mail, along with a few booklets. It seemed that I had to sell dozens of containers of this hand cream in order to win the "super" prizes I was clamoring for. Once again, I was the laughing-stock of my whole family. While they did help me out by buying a few containers of hand cream, they basically felt that I was foolish for sending the money with the hope of getting the prizes. What was worse was that the company continued to send me more and more hand cream. I had dozens of jars of this stuff within a month. Finally, my father wrote them a letter and explained that I was five, with little sales experience, and that we wanted to return the mer-chandise and get our money back.

When I got a little older and was concerned about the size of my muscles, I responded to one of those classic Charles Atlas adver-tisements. While a bully had never kicked sand in my face, I thought I ought to be ready for any sneak attack from this kind of brute.

As you can see, advertising and the mass media had a powerful impact on my life. These early experiences probably marked the start of my interest in advertising and entrepreneurship. Think about the powerful effect television and the comic book advertisements had on me. Each of the messages appealed to my fantasy life in a compelling way. These advertisements and commercials presented me with a big promise. They made me an offer that I simply could not refuse. While I am strongly opposed to the idea of duping or fooling children, I am fascinated with the power advertising can have over people who have a lot more common sense and life experience than does a young child.

WHY AM I TELLING YOU ALL THIS?

There are really two reasons. First, if this book is to have the personal tone that my editor and I favor, I think it is helpful if you know a bit about me. Second, if you want to understand how advertising and the media work, think about the impact they have had– and continue to have–on you and your family. What ads do you recall? Which ones have you responded to? Which messages do you despise? Which commercials have influenced the way you think about the world? Which do you love to watch or read over and over again?

If you want to create effective advertisements for your business or venture, you need to become a bit of a sales psychologist. In other words, you have to study the pitches contained in other messages and ascertain why and how they affected you or the target audience for which they are intended. Take note of the advertisements or commercials that caused you to think, behave, or feel a particular way. Consider which messages you remember of the thousands of pieces of communication you have been exposed to. Take a look at the award-winning ads in your industry or profession and try to understand what makes them so special. If you watched television or listened to the radio last night, which commercials, if any, do you remember?

In short, in order to develop persuasive sales messages for your business, or to work effectively with an advertising agency or consultant, you must begin to closely examine the content and nature of the effective sales messages that have an impact on you and those around you. Advertising is now such a large part of our daily experiences that we often do not notice the subtle ways it might affect us. Nevertheless, if you want to use advertising in an effective manner in the 1990s, you must learn how these messages affect not only yourself but also those you wish to communicate with about your products, your ideas, or your company.

Chapter 3

Entrepreneurial Advertising:
Some Business Basics
and a Lot of Common Sense

While this book is primarily about advertising, I would be remiss if I did not say a few words about the role of planning and its links with the creation of effective sales messages and marketing campaigns. In many respects, developing advertising for an older, established company is far easier than it is to create effective advertising for a new venture. Established industries and companies have years of experience and data from which they can learn a great deal. There are hundreds of business plans, advertising plans, marketing plans, research articles, and case examples that act as road maps for the advertising and promotional efforts of companies with some history behind them. It's quite different for the entrepreneur who frequently breaks ground and travels in uncharted territories. He or she must often rely on intuition, common sense, and whatever knowledge that can be obtained from related industries and similar ventures.

Since entrepreneurs are frequently breaking new ground, they often mistake one kind of business problem for another. For example, many entrepreneurs have asked for my help with their advertising or public relations when, in fact, what they needed was a better business plan or marketing scheme. Often, the person who is launching a new venture is somewhat unclear about the exact direction and course the business will take. It is also quite common for the start-up business person to do things in a somewhat disorganized and chaotic manner. In their eagerness to get their ventures rolling, many entrepreneurs shoot from the hip when making their initial business decisions. I know. I've done this myself.

Jackson (1991) has put forth five essentials that he feels must be met if you are to have a successful idea for a profitable business of your own:

1. A product or service that produces substantially more value for the customer than it costs and that can be produced or delivered for significantly less than it sells for.
2. A conscious, tested way to communicate this value to potential customers in a way that cost-effectively creates sales.
3. A management or manager willing to set up and observe objective criteria for measuring performance against a predetermined plan–and to let go of ideas that demonstrably aren't working.
4. An organized, clear, time-oriented, truthful business plan that sets out specific goals and timetables, and an accurate, realistic budget reviewed by an accountant.
5. Enough money to carry you through your business plan, even if 50% of your goals are not met on time.

According to Jackson, if any of these essential conditions are not met, you must carefully reconsider your business idea.

Developing your advertising before you have a solid business plan is a good example of doing things backwards. This kind of poor planning can cost you a lot of time, money, and energy and it can produce all kinds of headaches and hassles for you. Take it from someone who has, on occasion, forged ahead without doing enough research and planning. It is much wiser to slow down and do things in a pragmatic, well-organized, and sensible manner. I will tell you more about some of my own mistakes when I discuss some of my successes and failures later on. For now, take my advice and avoid this potentially fatal error. Get a sound business plan before you begin to deal with your company's advertising plan.

WHERE CAN YOU GO FOR HELP WITH YOUR BUSINESS PLAN?

There are a number of good books, computer programs, and video cassettes to assist entrepreneurs and small business owners in developing a business plan for their company's development. A company called JAIN has a software package (BizPlan Builder) that can help you answer a lot of the right questions and develop the written materials that comprise a typical business plan. A computer program of this kind can be quite valuable in assisting you with the planning of your venture. In many instances, these programs will point out problems and issues you may not have considered on your own. In addition, they can help you prepare an attractive document, which you will undoubtedly need if you plan to raise money from outside sources.

Also, lawyers, accountants, bankers, universities, and business consultants who specialize in working with entrepreneurs and the Small Business Administration can be valuable sources for information on business planning and the writing of a business plan.

As I mentioned earlier, writing a thorough business plan will help you to address many questions and potential problems you may have overlooked. In the long run, a good business plan will help you to save more money, raise more money, and make more money. A sound business plan also drives and guides your marketing, advertising, and promotional efforts and enables you to produce more effective advertisements, direct mail campaigns, brochures, and commercials.

Once your business plan is in place and you are up and running (or about to launch your venture), there are a number of ideas you should bear in mind before producing any advertising copy or promotional materials.

ENTREPRENEURIAL ADVERTISING AND CORPORATE ADVERTISING

Many textbooks and corporate types are proponents of the idea that advertising is primarily about achieving communication goals and enhancing a product's image. For the entrepreneur, however, advertising is most often about getting the message out, usually quickly, and generating more sales leads and–hopefully–sales. For the aggressive entrepreneur, in many instances, advertising is basically about selling.

Prior to the development of the electronic media, advertising was described as salesmanship in print. Today, it is useful for entrepreneurs and small business owners to think of advertising as being salesmanship in either the print or electronic media.

ADVERTISING, SELLING, AND PSYCHOLOGY

In order to be an effective salesperson, you have got to get inside the head of your target audience. You've got to become a bit of an industrial psychologist and know how your audience thinks, feels, eats, sleeps, drinks, and breathes. You need to know what they do for fun, whom they vote for, what books they read, what shows and events they watch on television, what they dream about, what they worry about, what they like, what they don't like, when they will resist your message, and when they will respond positively to what you have to say. You need to know how old they are, what sex they are, where their ancestors came from, and whether they pray in a church, synagogue, or mosque.

The research people call this information psychographics and demographics. Entrepreneurs call it knowing your customer. There are a number of ways you can acquire this information without doing expensive and time-consuming market research. Start by identifying who your target audience is most likely to be. You can do this by thinking about past customers and by talking to potential customers.

Realize that selecting the target audience is not always as simple as it may appear to be. For instance, while men are the main users of men's cologne, a lot of the buying is actually done by females who are buying presents for their husbands, lovers, fiances, brothers, or fathers. Remember, users may not always be consumers, and vice versa. Similarly, the people who do the purchasing are often influenced by other family members. How often do you see children in supermarkets saying, "Mommy, I want this cereal. I saw it on television." And frequently, the parent complies with the child's request. In brief, consider the nature of the person who makes the purchases as well as the individuals and groups that shape the buyer's consumer behavior.

In many instances, you will be able to learn a lot about your target audience from trade journals, industry associations, government publications, and business indexes. There are also many useful reference books on virtually every industry at your local university library.

PEOPLE, BUYING BEHAVIOR, AND ADVERTISING

There are hundreds of books on consumer behavior that can teach you a lot about the psychological and sociological factors that influence purchasing decisions. As I mentioned earlier, I have a PhD in counseling-psychology and have worked as a psychotherapist for 12 years. My experiences with clients have taught me a great deal about the way people think, behave, feel, and make decisions. In addition, I have learned a great deal about human nature, what troubles people, what makes them feel good, what they dream about, what they love, what they fear, what motivates them to change, what keeps them from changing, and how they deal with all of life's interpersonal dilemmas.

It will probably come as no surprise that many people look to the media and advertising to find solutions to a wide range of psychological and emotional problems. The adolescent who is concerned about his or her complexion is apt to be very intrigued with a message for a new acne remedy. What can the advertiser say to get the teenager interested in this particular remedy? The man or woman who is trying to lose weight is confronted with thousands of messages for diets, diet products, exercise devices, weight control programs, diet aids, health spas, and weight control programs. How can advertisers for this huge array of products and services get people to attend to their message and select their particular product or service?

No matter what you are advertising or selling, you are faced with motivational questions of this kind all the time. "What is the right appeal for my product?" "What button do we need to push to get through to our audience?" "What form and media are likely to have the most desirable impact on the people we want to reach?"

RATIONAL vs. EMOTIONAL APPEALS

One of the oldest debates in the advertising game is whether people buy for logical and pragmatic reasons or for crazy reasons that are driven by illogical fantasies housed in a wild and rather unpredictable unconscious mind. Some people believe that we make big decisions on an emotional basis and support these decisions with facts. My own feeling is that human beings buy for both reasons. There is no question that almost all of us will buy an inexpensive impulse item on a whim because it appeals to some fleeting feeling that exists within us at a given moment. Picking up a T-shirt with a logo from a sporting event or concert is frequently not a logical or carefully planned decision. Likewise, many consumers buy magazines like *People* and *The National Enquirer* on impulse. They begin to browse through the magazine while they wait in the check-out line at the market. While they are watching their groceries move forward on the conveyer belt, the copy or photo on the cover captures their attention and induces them to open the magazine. They begin to get interested in the material and they decide to throw it in with the rest of the groceries. After all, what's another buck or two when you've spent $100 on feeding the family?

If you analyze this small piece of consumer behavior, you can learn a great deal about advertising, selling, and psychology. People who pick up the tabloid are in an emotional state and are in need of some intrigue, adventure, romance, or titillation. They have just spent the better part of an hour waiting at the deli counter and the bakery. If that weren't enough, they have had four collisions with other shoppers' carts and had to keep one eye on the shopping list and the other eye on little Jimmy or Jane who is trying to grab everything on every shelf in the supermarket. Given this kind of frustration, plus the stress and fatigue of cruising the supermarket aisles, it's small wonder that there are any copies of the tabloids left in the supermarket check-out racks.

This kind of impulse purchase is very different from buying a high-ticket item like a car or appliance. The consumer psychology is very different in these situations. In fact, it is not uncommon for some consumers to spend months researching the products in a given category when it comes to a substantial purchase of this kind. Although some consumers appear to buy a car in a rather pragmatic way, there is a lot of illogical behavior surrounding this decision as well. For instance, some consumers are clearly driven by the image they feel the car will project about them. For example, I know a number of middle-aged men who have bought sports cars because they believe the car helps them to look and feel younger. The automobile, for some people in their forties or fifties, is a quick fix for a mid-life crisis. Other kinds of bizarre behavior transpire in automobile showrooms. Have you ever noticed how many men turn on the radio as soon as they test-drive a car? It is difficult to check out the engine and ride when the sound system is blasting; nevertheless, this is what many male consumers do. It is curious behavior indeed when you consider the fact that people are spending $15,000 to $50,000 on radios when it appeared that they were trying to buy an automobile.

Buying an engagement ring is another purchase that is loaded with psychological issues. The shape, size, and cost of the stone have a slew of psychological ramifications for both the bride and the groom. Sigmund Freud and his disciples could have a field day analyzing the symbolic meanings of the engagement ring to the newlyweds. Observe the way a couple shops for a ring and you can learn a tremendous amount about the way our emotions and personalities affect our buying patterns. Sometimes the groom elects to surprise his bride-to-be. In other cases, the couple visit the jewelry shops together. You can learn a great deal about buying behavior and the human psyche by listening to the questions people ask about the diamond, as well as noticing how they look at it. Observe the way they decide on shape, price, setting, and style, and how or if they renegotiate the price. Notice the role that each member of the dyad assumes in the buying decision.

As I said earlier, some consumer decisions are both rational and emotional. For example, someone may buy a suit because it carries a respected name brand and "feels good." Other consumers who are more cost-conscious will remain loyal to a brand simply because of price.

My father-in-law, who was in the textile business for many years, shed some light on the ways many of his customers would purchase the elastic his company manufactured. One particular customer was infamous for trying to lower his costs by using less material and elastic in some of the clothing he produced. When he heard the high cost of the elastic for one order, he remarked, "Take from the crotch! Take from the crotch! You'll have to take some material from the crotch!" Purchasing decisions in the textile business are frequently made on the basis of three factors–price, price, and price. In this highly competitive industry, speed of delivery and quality seem to be far less important in most instances.

While the focus of this book is on consumer advertising, some of these same principles apply to business-to-business advertising and selling as well. To some extent, it doesn't matter what business you are in or who your customer is. If you are going to be successful, you have to observe the way people behave in stores. Listen to the conversations they have with salespeople. Notice when they become interested and when they become resistant or defensive. Take a look at the expressions on their faces when they respond to an in-store display, when they pick up an item from the shelf or a rack, and when they reach into their wallet or pocketbook for their cash or credit card. Also, observe your own shopping behavior and your own responses to sales messages. Whenever I stay on the phone with a telemarketing person for more than ten seconds, I always try to sort out what they said that kept me from hanging up on them. There is much that an entrepreneur can learn from observing master salespeople and shoppers in action.

There is also a wealth of information you can utilize from your present customers and business contacts. I recently received a phone call from a client of mine who had sent a direct mail piece describing his employee assistance program. His piece was sent to several hundred human resource directors in medium-sized corporations. After the mailing, he was able to schedule meetings with ten of these key decision makers. Unfortunately, he did not make a sale. He called me up because he was disappointed and frustrated. I encouraged him to hang in there and I explained that part of being an entrepreneur is learning how to develop creative solutions to a wide array of business problems. In addition, I suggested that he contact each of the people he had met with to find out why they did not purchase his services. My guess is that this young man and his associate need to establish a bit more credibility in their fields and sharpen their selling skills in order to secure contracts with the corporations they have targeted. They probably need to do some lecturing, write journal articles, and present papers at seminars or conventions. In the interim, however, I believe he will learn a great deal if he constructs a brief questionnaire aimed at identifying the nature of his potential customers' resistance to his pitch.

It doesn't matter if you are growing a business or running an established corporation; you have got to interview present and past customers and find out how they feel about you, your product, your advertising, and your company. If you like, you can develop a survey that will help you identify your strengths and weaknesses, your competition's strengths and weaknesses, potentially effective advertising appeals, and your strongest selling points. Ask people why they chose you or what would compel them to buy your product instead of your competitor's. Talk to your competitor's customers and find out why they can't be your customers. Find out what they think about your advertising. Which messages do they like best, and why? Determine which ones they recall and which they have never noticed or have forgotten.

Despite all the fuss over sophisticated market research, I believe that it is pretty simple to get a handle on who your best potential customers are and what is the best way to communicate with them. While it may be a little bit more difficult to acquire this information if you're starting a new venture, this is the kind of data that successful heads of companies usually possess about their customers. As one chief executive officer recently told me, "You have got to get into your stores and be with your customers to really know what the hell is happening with your business."

As I mentioned earlier, if you are starting a venture, it is not always that simple to determine who your customer is going to be. However, in order to decide upon your most likely target audience, you may find it helpful to answer a few very basic questions:

1. What business am I in?
2. Who can most benefit from my product or service?
3. How far away are the people who are apt to be my customers?
4. Are there enough potential customers in my area to support this venture?
5. How can I describe these people in terms of age, sex, income level, media habits, lifestyle, and fantasies?

6. Do I envision expanding into other areas or other product lines?
7. Who is my competition?
8. Who are their customers?
9. What is the best way to reach these customers with my messages?
10. What will compel people to use or switch to my product?

CUSTOMER ESSAYS

Another good way to learn about what makes your customer or potential customer tick is to write what I call the customer paragraph or customer essay. This paragraph is written from the user's, consumer's, or key decision maker's point of view. These essays tend to help the entrepreneur get inside his audience's mind and get a better understanding of how they think, feel, and behave. It's a little like running a focus group, without going to the trouble and expense of putting the panel together. This exercise also helps you get a sense of the way your customers speak and hear. You get a feeling for their language. Remember, construction workers tend to speak very differently from housewives. Similarly, physicians have a different kind of vocabulary and mindset than do auto mechanics. Likewise, people from different ethnic backgrounds tend to structure their dialogues in different ways.

Customer essays can also be quite helpful in developing headlines, slogans, and concepts for your advertisements, commercials, and direct mail pieces. The following is a sample of a customer essay for a new golf gadget:

> I've been playing this game for ten years now. I'm a real duffer. I hardly ever break one hundred. I've spent a fortune on golf lessons, golf schools, golf books, and golf gadgets. You name it, if it has to do with golf, I've bought it. I will do anything to improve my game. I'd do anything if I could add twenty yards to my tee shot and keep the ball on the fairway. You know, I joke about it, but I'm sick of my buddies beating me every week. I don't bet much on our Sunday game, but I must have lost about five hundred bucks this season alone! I

wish I could find a club or a device that would get me on the right track.

Here's a customer paragraph for a person who is looking for a new law firm:

> I can't believe this last bill. This firm is charging me a fortune and I can never get my attorney to return my phone calls. I have been with this firm for a few years, but I think it's time for a change. We're being charged too much money for too little service. Besides, they always seem to be putting junior associates on our company's legal matters. These kids are fresh out of law school and they never know what's going on. Yep. It is definitely time for a change. One of the guys I play tennis with has a law firm he is really happy with. I'm going to give him a call and get his lawyer's name.

If you write and read your customer essays carefully, you will discover lots of ideas for headlines, copy points, and even visuals to accompany the copy.

COLLEAGUES AND COMPETITORS: A GOLD MINE OF INFORMATION

In the same way you become a student of consumer behavior, you must also become a student of your industry or business. You must learn all you can from those around you who are in similar or related industries. While it is unlikely that the person who is in the same business down the street from you will share trade secrets with you, someone running the same kind of company in another region may be more than happy to share ideas with you. You can make contact with a lot of individuals who can, and will, help you at conferences, conventions, trade shows, and trade associations.

As far as your competitors are concerned, it is important that you be cognizant of what they are doing with regard to pricing, planning, marketing, advertising, public relations, distribution, and the development of new products. In some instances, your advertising will be shaped by what your competitor does or does not do. Consider the ongoing competition between companies like Hertz and Avis and Ford's Truck Division and Chevrolet's Truck Division.

Remember, if you're an entrepreneur, it is vital that you get as much information about your customers and competition as possible. If you don't have your hand on the pulses of your competitors and customers, you will be shooting from the hip when you launch your advertising. You might even be successful if your instincts are sharp. However, you will flip the odds in your favor significantly and leave less to chance if you do your homework and learn all you can about your target audience and others in your industry.

KNOW YOUR PRODUCT

You need to know as much about your product, service, or business as you do about your customer and your competition. This should not be much of a problem for most entrepreneurs since they frequently are the ones who have invented or conceptualized the product or business. Nevertheless, make certain that you know about the product's strengths and weaknesses, its quality, the materials used in its construction, its history, its future, planned modifications, related products, planned line extensions, etc. Make a list of ten reasons for buying your product instead of your competitor's.

Once you have a handle on your customers, your competition, and your product or products, you will discover some very important relationships among these three factors. Your advertising should be designed to communicate the important facts, benefits, and advantages that your product or company offers to your target users. After reflecting on the nature of your product and your customer, you may discover a unique link between your company and your target audience. If you have, you may be on to what advertising people call "the big idea."

I first heard the term "big idea" when I was enrolled in an advertising course at New York University a number of years ago. The teacher asked the students to write an advertisement for a product we often used. I am an avid tennis player, and I frequently use a grip tape on my racket. I find this very helpful because it absorbs perspiration, builds up the size of my grip a bit, and also prevents blisters (particularly at the start of the tennis season). I played up the latter benefit and came up with the headline "Bandage Your Racket Instead Of Your Hand." This lead line seemed to make sense because the grip tape was put on in the same manner as a bandage might be applied to one's hand. Blisters are a problem for many tennis players, and this was a clever way to communicate one of the product's main benefits. In any event, the instructor loved the idea and said, "Jay, you have come up with what we call a big idea."

The "big idea" offers consumers a dynamic and compelling reason to choose your product or company over your competitor's. A smart entrepreneur is always on the lookout for this kind of concept. You will hear more about the importance of the "big idea" later.

WHAT PROBLEMS DO YOU WANT
YOUR ADVERTISING TO SOLVE?

In order to best determine the content, tone, and nature of your sales messages, it is important for you to decide exactly what you want your advertising to do for your company. While the answer to these questions seems quite simple and straightforward, many business owners fail to realize the range of functions that advertising can perform for their ventures besides getting more customers and increasing sales. Furthermore, entrepreneurs sometimes hope their advertising will solve a problem that has nothing to do with promotional efforts. For instance, some entrepreneurs confuse an advertising problem with a management issue. A few brief anecdotes will show you what I mean.

Several years ago, I was asked to visit a law firm in order to advise them on their advertising campaign and help them generate more new clients. The firm's present campaign did not seem that bad to me. But after doing a little investigating, I determined that the problem had much more to do with the firm's receptionist than with its newspaper, radio, or Yellow Pages campaign. You see, the person who answers the phone in this kind of business is the link between new clients and the attorneys. Consequently, this individual must have an excellent phone personality and be quite adept at establishing a relationship with the caller and channeling the call to the appropriate attorney. Unfortunately, this firm's receptionist had a personality like Attila the Hun. She was incredibly cold and was basically defeating the whole purpose of the advertising campaign. My recommendation to the senior partners of this firm was to train her in customer service, get her a new personality, or replace her with someone who could manage phone calls in a more congenial and civilized manner. In this instance, the problem was more of a managerial and personnel nature than an advertising issue.

While working on another account, I produced a radio campaign that generated more inquiries than one entrepreneur could handle. He simply lacked the manpower and phone power to handle all the feedback his campaign generated.

I can also recall working with a client who had run a very successful fresh fruit and vegetable stand for many years. She was so good at running this business that she decided to open a retail fruit and vegetable business that would carry more products than her stand did and that would also provide gourmet catering and create gift baskets. This entrepreneur contacted me because she wanted to expand the catering component of her new retail store.

I developed a very successful print campaign that generated lots of calls and a fair amount of business in a short period of time. (In fact, I have thought about syndicating these advertisements so that other caterers around the country could use them.) The campaign consisted of three small advertisements that ran in the Wednesday food section and the Sunday entertainment section of local newspapers. The ads included photos of the owner, with her fruits and vegetables in the background. The attractive and very likeable owner was well-known in the county, so it seemed like a good idea to capitalize on her image.

Although my client got a lot of calls, some new business, and an abundance of positive feedback from her advertising campaign, the communications program could not overcome her difficulties with her new partner (who was also the chef), her inability to fill her catering orders promptly, and the increased taxes, costs, and overhead that accompanied her new retail location. In spite of the fact that I had developed a successful advertising program for this businesswoman, it seemed that she lacked the wherewithal to run this catering business. As it turns out, she closed the store, left me with an unpaid bill of about $1700, and returned to her fruit stand.

In another instance, the president of a large private university asked me what could be done to resolve the school's declining enrollment. After doing a little research on this problem, I discovered that many universities were experiencing a drop in enrollments due to changing demographic conditions, a widespread recession, and a decrease in corporate endowments and private donations to many institutions. I gave the president an idea for an advertisement, which was subsequently used in a slightly different form. However, the president did not have an adequate budget to run the ad often enough in order for it to be effective. Also, the president, while a very nice fellow, was totally out of touch with the students, the faculty, the trustees, and the widespread problems facing the university. He spent money on foolish and poorly conceived projects and had little insight into how to market and build a university in a highly competitive environment. In short, it was simply unreasonable to assume that an advertising campaign could resolve these kinds of widespread management and financial problems.

The moral of these stories: You need to be a good manager and planner as well as a good advertiser in order to succeed in any venture. Furthermore, these cases illustrate the importance of viewing your advertising in the context of the *whole* business. As I suggested earlier, advertising campaigns can perform a variety of functions for a new venture, a growing business, or an established corporation: They can attract new customers; remind old customers of you and your business; combat some bad publicity; announce a sale; announce a new product; turn a disadvantage into an advantage; lengthen a buying season; increase brand preference; increase market share; announce the opening of a new business, branch, or location; communicate the differences between your product and the competition's; encourage people to buy an item in greater quantity or frequency; motivate a sales force; generate leads for salespeople; increase the number of different users of your product; reposition your product or company; motivate customers to switch brands; announce a sale or support a promotion; enhance a company's image or reputation; conduct research for future campaigns;

test an idea or new product; or disseminate additional information about your firm, product, or service.

Many entrepreneurs make the mistake of launching an advertising campaign that lacks a clear focus and quantifiable objectives. Consequently, the entrepreneur must think about and carefully plan what problem each component of the campaign is to solve and how each component can best work together. For example, a print campaign advertising a sale may be integrated with a radio and billboard program designed to reinforce the company's name or image.

SETTING ADVERTISING OBJECTIVES

Once the functions of the campaign have been clearly identified, quantifiable objectives for measuring the impact and effectiveness of the program should be established. These objectives can include an increase in name awareness; an increase in inquiries from distributors about your product; an increase in sales; an increase in sales in new markets or among new users; opening of new locations; improved recall of a new advertisement compared with an old one; increased productivity on the part of the sales force; and a gain in market share.

Whatever objectives you choose, they must be clear and easy to quantify or measure in some way. If you like, you can measure the number of new customers you get in one year, the number of units you sell, an increase in store traffic, an increase in leads, or a host of other variables. Setting these kinds of parameters will help you effectively monitor your advertising's impact on your business's growth.

Chapter 4

Persuading Customers

All successful communication is hypnosis.

–Milton Erickson, M.D.

Now that I have reviewed a few business basics and spoken about the importance of knowing your product, your customer, and your competition, we can start to deal with the question of how you go about getting potential customers to attend to your sales messages and how you can persuade the people you want to influence.

WHAT IS PERSUASION?

When you think of persuasion, a lot of different thoughts, words, and concepts probably come to mind: influencing others, manipulating people, controlling decisions, shaping attitudes, subliminal messages, brainwashing, coercion, and closing deals. The entrepreneur who is building a company is often the person who "sells" his or her company to bankers, investors, and customers. The successful business owner is often someone who knows how to convince people to do what they might be reluctant or ambivalent about doing. These are the kinds of people whom it is difficult to say no to.

The adroit business person knows how to read people and how to charm them. He or she knows how to make a lasting impression at meetings, dinner parties, and trade shows. He or she understands how to motivate people, how to remove defenses and barriers, eliminate resistance, and cajole people into acting or responding in a desired manner. The competent entrepreneur searches for the right button to push to get through to people. He or she tries to determine the right appeal, content, and tone of his or her written and oral messages. The clever entrepreneur tries to entertain clients and potential clients in a way that will be meaningful, enjoyable, and memorable for these important individuals. The savvy business person may use certain words and expressions with some people in order to strengthen a relationship with them.

At times, the entrepreneur may model or imitate the pace at which a person speaks in order to put himself or herself on the same wavelength with the person he or she wants to influence or persuade. That is, the skilled entrepreneur is often an adept communicator as well as an insightful psychologist. Realize that if your advertising is to be successful, it must accomplish many of the same things that the skilled entrepreneur achieves in face-to-face meetings with other decision makers. You must also remember that most people really don't give a damn about your advertising. While you might spend hours agonizing over your mission statement, your headline, and your slogan, the rest of the people on the planet care very little about these matters.

As I explain to college students who enroll in my copywriting course, writing advertising is very much like any other situation in life where you find yourself trying to get through to someone who may have little interest in you or what you are about to say. In order to demonstrate this situation to young people, who are in many ways unsophisticated about communication strategies, I ask my students to consider the following scenario:

You're at a party and you notice someone who is really attractive. You've spotted the person from across the room and you can sense that electricity. Your heart rate accelerates. As your eyes fixate on the person, you notice that he or she is talking to someone else. You continue to watch from a distance. Suddenly, it looks like your love from afar is getting ready to leave.

If you don't make your move now, you will lose your chance to make contact with the person, and the opportunity to meet Mr./Ms. Right will pass you by.

What can you say or do in a few seconds that will get this person's attention? What can you do to encourage the person to stay a little longer and talk to you for a few moments? You must say or do something that will get you noticed. You must have an approach that is memorable but sincere. You can't make a fool of yourself. That could ruin your chances of getting to know this person (as well as other people on campus). Do you think you should use a hard sell or a soft sell? Does the person seem shy or outgoing? What kinds of words do you think will get a response? What can you learn from the person's mannerisms, body language, and gestures that will tell you how to communicate most effectively? Should you start with a joke, a compliment, or should you begin with a catchy remark like, "I have been looking at you for ten minutes and trying to figure out what I could say to meet you before you leave."

This situation is very similar to the quandary copywriters face every day. Whenever you are preparing an advertisement, you are constantly faced with a few simple but important questions that will be discussed repeatedly in this book:

1. What can I do or say to get people to notice this message?
2. What can I do or say to get people to listen to, watch, or read this message?
3. What can I do or say to create a positive feeling about my business?
4. What can I do or say to get people to remember the message and my company?
5. What can be done to set this business apart from the competition?
6. What is the most unique benefit I can communicate about my business?
7. What is the best tone for my message: friendly, factual, humorous, conversational, authoritative, low key, entertaining, upbeat, or some combination of the above?

Since I am a psychotherapist by training, I tend to view advertising from a psychological viewpoint much of the time. When a business client asks me to write an advertisement, I am always trying to get a sense of what will motivate potential customers to be interested in a particular message, a particular company, or a particular offer. In addition, I frequently begin the creative process by considering what I can do or say to get the reader's, viewer's, or listener's undivided attention.

When practicing psychotherapy, the clinician is always searching for strategies and techniques that will make patients more aware of themselves, their relationships, and their environments. In order to heighten a patients' awareness and increase their insight into themselves, the therapist may use a range of techniques. For example, the psychologist may ask the person a question the individual has never considered before (e.g., "What was the happiest moment in your life?" or "What would your life be like if you woke up fifty pounds lighter tomorrow morning?")

Skilled therapists try to get people to perceive their life situations differently in order to get their undivided attention, intensify their awareness of options in situations which often appear to be hopeless, and facilitate behavioral and attitudinal change.

For instance, some years ago a woman in her late twenties came to see me because she had great difficulty losing weight. She had tried many diet programs but was never able to stick with them for any length of time.

After a few sessions, it became quite apparent to me and to this patient that she was afraid to lose her excess weight because she was quite frightened of the male attention and intimacy which she might experience if she were to become more attractive.

This woman had seen her parents' marriage collapse as a child and had been abandoned by her father after the divorce. Her mother repeatedly communicated the idea that men could not be trusted. These messages exacerbated her daughter's fear, suspicion, and lack of trust in men.

During our third meeting, I suggested that this young woman really work hard and take the weight off just one time. I reassured her that if she did not like how she looked and felt and did not care for the attention that she received, she could always put the weight back on. I also reminded her of the health benefits that go along with having a leaner body. I spoke about the dangers of heart disease, diabetes, and other physical ailments. Furthermore, I explained that together we could handle any difficulties she might encounter once she got rid of those unwanted pounds and inches.

Once she felt that she could reverse a potentially frightening situation, this patient felt comfortable enough to lose fifty pounds in four months. More important, she is now involved in a meaningful relationship and has kept the excess weight off for many years.

Like advertisers and entrepreneurs, psychologists are always seeking more effective and powerful ways to communicate with people. In some cases psychologists, psychiatrists, counselors, and psychotherapists utilize hypnosis and hypnotic techniques to communicate more effectively with their patients and clients. As I remarked at the start of this book, I believe that good advertising has a great deal in common with hypnosis.

HYPNOTIC ADVERTISING

Some advertisements and commercials are so captivating, so engaging, and so fascinating that people enjoy reading, watching, and hearing them over and over again. These powerful messages can entertain, persuade, and motivate millions of people to feel, think, behave, and purchase differently. Conversely, other messages get lost in the media clutter and have little or no impact on anyone. Why do some advertisements have a profound impact on readers', viewers', and listeners' lives, while others are barely noticed? Why do people zap some commercials and enjoy watching other spots time and time again? Why are some small black-and-white advertisements clipped out of newspapers and magazines and saved for months, while other full-page, four-color messages are ignored by the same readers? Why do some sales messages induce a trance-like state on the part of the viewers or listeners, while others seem to compel people to go to the kitchen or call a friend?

Are the intense levels of interest and concentration that some messages produce similar to the trances induced by stage hypnotists, psychologists, or psychiatrists? How can hypnotic techniques be effectively incorporated into advertisements and commercials? What can entrepreneurs do to make certain that their advertising messages have the desired effect and impact on their respective target audiences? Some advertising experts have casually noted the connection between hypnosis and advertising. For example, Vance Packard (1957) mentions hypnosis several times in his book on advertising, *The Hidden Persuaders:* "Preliminary results seem to indicate that hypnosis helps in getting honest reasons for copy and brand preferences." Packard quotes a package design executive as saying, "You have to have a carton that attracts and hypnotizes this woman, like waving a flashlight in front of her eyes."

An advertising executive tells Packard: "We found that an exciting mystery show was inconsistent with the need to put the audience into the calm frame of mind necessary to receive and remember our . . . commercial."

Packard also details John Steinbeck's commentary on the relationship between hypnosis and political advertising in an article Steinbeck wrote for *The Saturday Review*: "The audience has been amused and half-hypnotized by a fat comedian. The time following such a program, [Steinbeck] said, 'is very valuable, for here you have X millions of people in a will-less, helpless state, unable to resist any suggestion offered. . . .' " According to Packard, James Vicary, a motivational analyst, theorized that people were often in a hypnotic state when they went shopping. Packard writes: "The ladies fell into a what Mr. Vicary calls a hypnoidal trance, a light kind of trance that, he explains, is the first stage of hypnosis. Mr. Vicary has decided that the main cause of the trance is that the supermarket is packed with products that in former years would have been items that only kings and queens could afford, and here in this fairyland they were available. Mr. Vicary theorizes: Just in this generation, anyone can be a king or queen and go through these stores where the products say 'buy me, buy me.' "

While these remarks identify potential uses of hypnosis in the advertising process, they merely begin to suggest how hypnotic techniques can help advertising practitioners to produce more persuasive and effective messages. No one has yet explored the fascinating and important relationships between advertising and hypnosis in detail. Moreover, no one has shown advertising professionals how they can use hypnotic strategies and techniques to solve a wide range of complex business communication problems. Similarly, while there are dozens of books on effective advertising techniques, theories, and strategies, few have addressed the manner in which advertising practitioners and entrepreneurs can benefit from a better understanding of hypnosis, hypnotic techniques, and self-hypnosis.

Likewise, while much has been written on hypnotism, hypnosis, and self-hypnosis and their applications in sports psychology, counseling, psychotherapy, pain management, and the treatment of anxiety, phobias, and insomnia, very little information has been disseminated on the vital role hypnosis plays in the advertising process.

The following pages will provide you with an overview of hypnosis and the important role it plays in many aspects of advertising. Moreover, this section will point out the numerous parallels between the advertising process and the hypnotic experience and show how some of the most effective advertisements and commercials of all time rely on hypnotic techniques, methods, and strategies. (Realize that this is not to say that every effective commercial places people in a trance. I am merely stating that there are many similarities between the way trances are induced and the ways in which sales messages impact their audiences.) Later on in this book, I will also show you how hypnosis can enhance the creative ideation that is vital for entrepreneurs as well as art directors, creative directors, copywriters, chief executive officers, and strategic planners. In addition, you will learn how and why advertisers can benefit from utilizing the same methods of persuasion employed by clinical psychologists, psychiatrists, stage hypnotists, ministers, politicians, professors, attorneys, and salespeople.

WHAT IS HYPNOSIS?

When hypnosis or hypnotism is mentioned, many people think of the stage hypnotist who, after placing a subject in a deep trance, persuades this individual to engage in an absurd task or act in order to amaze and entertain an audience. However, the stage hypnotist is usually dealing with subjects who are very willing participants and who are capable of achieving a rather deep trance. Moreover, stage hypnosis is merely one example of the many forms of all these phenomena. It is more important and significant to note that we all experience hypnosis or self-hypnosis almost every day of our lives. Have you ever had a daydream or gotten so absorbed in a television program that you did not hear your spouse calling your name? Do you find yourself experiencing the so-called "runner's high" after you have been jogging for fifteen minutes? How many times have you driven to work on a highway and been so lost in your thoughts that you wondered how you arrived at your destination? It may feel as if your automobile were running on automatic pilot.

If you have ever lapsed into a daydream while attending a class or a business meeting and felt like you were there, but somehow not there, you were experiencing a form of hypnosis. Have you ever observed young people dancing to rock and roll music? If you look carefully, you will notice that many of them are in a hypnotic or trance-like state. There is a complete lack of expression on their faces and they often do not speak. Interestingly, many priests and witch doctors of primitive races induce hypnosis with chanting, dancing, music, and drum beats (LeCron, 1971). Similarly, if you observe children at a circus, you will notice the wide-eyed expression they have on their faces. These youngsters are frequently so focused on the spectacle that they forget about more mundane things like hot dogs, souvenirs, and cotton candy. People are also likely to slip into hypnosis during a movie, while at work, while engaging in a hobby, during an interesting lecture, while listening to music, while playing video games, while observing a sporting event, or while attending a religious ceremony.

The term hypnosis, originally derived from the Greek word for sleep, *hypnos,* has been defined and described differently by a number of different writers. For example, Weitzenhoffer (1957) described hypnosis as a condition or state of selective hyper-suggestibility brought about in an individual through the use of certain psychological manipulations.

John Yates, a psychiatrist who has written a self-help guide on hypnosis, defines it as an altered state of consciousness attainable by almost anyone. This altered state is characterized by increased concentration, distraction from the ordinary thinking process, and cooperation either with oneself or another person (Yates and Wallace, 1984).

Drs. Donald Moine and Kenneth Lloyd, two sales psychologists who have written a book on hypnotic selling, describe hypnosis as a state of greatly increased suggestibility in which the person is far more susceptible to influence by messages and images (Moine and Lloyd, 1990).

Leslie LeCron (1971), a clinical psychologist, views hypnosis as an altered state of consciousness and altered state of awareness, although the conscious mind is still present. During a non-hypnotic state, the waking mind is at the forefront. During hypnosis, the subconscious mind is most active and the conscious part of the mind is less active. In addition, during hypnosis, thoughts from the unconscious mind tend to move into consciousness.

Yapko (1990) defines hypnosis as any effective form of communication. This definition points out an important connection between advertising and hypnosis.

Seymour Frank, a salesman and professional hypnotist who utilizes hypnotic techniques in order to increase his sales, believes that hypnosis and salesmanship are closely related (Moine and Lloyd, 1990). According to Frank, "The hypnotist and the sales person both introduce their topic. They explain it, make the other party comfortable, and condition and cajole their 'subject' to do what they wish. They parry and thrust and ultimately, when they're good, they 'close.' " Frank finds that the salesperson and hypnotist have a great deal in common. That is, the hypnotist and the salesperson both offer benefits to their audiences. They both rely on simple, direct, and clear communication that contains "power phrases" intended to have a positive impact on the client. Frank also believes that hypnosis and sales are virtually the same:

> I do know, from my experience as both a professional hypnotist and a professional insurance salesman, that the two have much in common–from the opening to the close of their performance. And what combination is more logical? Hypnotism and sales have much in common because they are both forms of persuasive communication, and persuasive communication is salesmanship. In addition, hypnotism is the selling of an idea to a subject to get the subject to do what you want him to do. In sales, you have to present an idea that's satisfactory to the prospect so that he'll part with his money to buy what you are selling. And, in both instances, the presentation is everything. (Moine and Lloyd, 1990)

Like hypnosis and salesmanship, advertising deals with persuasion and communication. In fact, as was noted earlier, some people think of advertising as being nothing more than salesmanship in the print or electronic media.

Facts and Myths About Hypnosis

Due to the manner in which hypnosis has been portrayed by the mass media, there seems to be much confusion about what hypnosis is and what it is not. If advertising practitioners are to be able to utilize hypnotic methods effectively, they must have a clear understanding of this phenomenon. For example, it is often thought that people will become unconscious when they are placed in a hypnotic trance. This actually never happens, even when the most hypnotizable people enter a deep trance. In addition, many people erroneously believe they will relinquish all of their control to the person who has hypnotized them. In reality, the person's willpower is not removed by hypnosis. Moreover, no one will do anything while in a hypnotic trance that is contrary to his/her moral code.

There is also much confusion about the nature of the hypnotic trance. That is, many people believe that a hypnotic trance involves unconsciousness, sleep, and amnesia. This, too, is simply not true. In fact, many people become more keenly aware of themselves and their surroundings during hypnosis. Hypnosis is usually characterized by bodily sensations of floating, lightness or heaviness, sinking, rocking, or swirling motions. In addition, the hypnotized person is apt to experience thoughts, fantasies, and images that are quite vivid and realistic. Sight, smell, taste, touch, and hearing are all reported as actual perceptions. As one hypnotized person remarked during a light trance, "I can feel the ocean breeze and smell the salt air." Furthermore, people often find that their subconscious mind becomes quite active and adept at solving a wide range of problems that seemed impossible to resolve in a non-hypnotic state. This phenomenon has important implications for advertising. (These implications will be discussed later in this book.)

According to Yates (1984), hypnotic trances can be divided into three types: light, medium, and heavy. The kind of hypnosis induced by advertisements and commercials, in most instances, would fall into the light category. As was stated earlier, people frequently enter hypnotic trances naturally and unknowingly during the course of a day. During a light trance, people tend to be calm and relaxed and they feel as if cares, pressures, and demands have been removed. Facial muscles relax, muscular tension decreases, and respiratory patterns even out and slow down. The heartbeat and blood pressure usually drop as the person becomes increasingly more relaxed. In addition, in light hypnosis, the person often feels as if he or she is daydreaming.

People in a medium-level trance are not distracted by outside disturbances, and they may exhibit a semi-glazed or unfocused look in their eyes. They may be involved in a task and unable to hear someone who is trying to get their attention. Medium-level hypnotic states can include deep levels of relaxation or a complete lack of awareness of the body. In the deepest levels of hypnosis, it is difficult to recall what has transpired during the trance. This phenomenon is referred to as "hypnotic amnesia." In this kind of trance, the person's ability to imagine is greatly enhanced. Athletes have utilized this kind of hypnosis to increase their abilities to perform. Instead of using anesthesia, surgeons have performed many operations while the patient was in deep hypnosis. While many people can achieve a very deep trance through self-hypnosis or hypnosis that is induced by a hypnotherapist, advertisements and commercials have the capacity to create a light or mild trance in many instances.

Who Can be Hypnotized?

There is also much confusion about who is hypnotizable and who is not. In general, 5 percent of the people are not hypnotizable; about 30 percent can enter a light trance; approximately 50 percent can reach a medium trance; and 14 percent can enter a deep stage of hypnosis.

Who Is a Good Hypnotic Subject?

According to Yates (1984), people who are intelligent are among the best hypnotic subjects. People who are curious, bright, and adaptable tend to be good candidates for formal or direct hypnosis. The ability to concentrate and to control distractibility is also important. Highly motivated and cooperative people who have a propensity for daydreaming, doodling, becoming "lost" in listening to music, reading, fantasizing, or pursuing such hypnotic activities as jogging, playing chess, and meditating are all good candidates for hypnosis. Obviously, it is these kinds of people who are the targets for an abundance of advertisements and commercials.

DIRECT HYPNOSIS

A hypnotist can induce a trance by utilizing direct or indirect hypnosis. Since many effective advertisements utilize components of one or both of these approaches, it is important for the reader to understand the differences and similarities between both methods. Direct hypnosis is frequently utilized by psychiatrists, psychologists, and stage hypnotists. While there are numerous induction techniques that involve deep breathing, focusing on a particular point, and attending to the hypnotist's voice and changing physical sensations, many hypnotherapists rely on approaches resembling the one described by Weitzenhoffer (1957):

> Keep your eyes on that little light and listen carefully to what I say. Your ability to be hypnotized depends entirely on your willingness to cooperate. It has nothing to do with your intelligence. As for your will-power, if you want you can remain awake all the time and pay no attention to me. In that case, you might make me look silly, but you are only wasting time. On the other hand, if you pay close attention to what I say, and follow what I tell you, you can easily learn to fall into a hypnotic sleep. In that case you will be helping this experiment and not wasting any time. Hypnosis is nothing fearful or mysterious. It is merely a state of strong interest in some particular thing. In a sense you are hypnotized whenever you see a good show and forget you are part of the audience, but instead feel you are part of the story. Your cooperation, your interest is what I ask you. Your ability to be hypnotized is a measure of your willingness to cooperate. Nothing will be done that will in any way cause you the least embarrassment.
> Now relax and make yourself entirely comfortable. Keep your eyes on that little light. Keep staring at it all the time.

Keep staring as hard as you can, as long as you can. Relax completely. Relax every part of your body. Relax the muscles of your leg. Relax the muscles in your arms. Make yourself perfectly comfortable. Let yourself be limp, limp, limp. Relax more and more, more and more. Relax completely. Relax completely. Your legs feel very heavy and limp, heavy and limp. Your arms are heavy, heavy, heavy, heavy as lead. Your whole body feels heavy, heavier and heavier. You feel tired and sleepy, tired and sleepy. You feel drowsy, and sleepy, drowsy and sleepy. Your breathing is slow and regular, slow and regular.

Your eyes are tired from staring. Your eyes are wet from straining. The strain in your eyes is getting greater, greater and greater. You would like to close your eyes and relax completely (but keep your eyes open just a little longer, just a little longer). You will soon reach your limit. The strain will be so great, your eyes will be so tired, your lids will become so heavy, your eyes will close of themselves, close of themselves. And then you will be completely relaxed, completely relaxed. Warm and comfortable, warm and comfortable. Tired and drowsy. Tired and sleepy. Sleepy. Sleepy. Sleepy. You are paying attention to nothing but the sound of my voice. You hear nothing but the sound of my voice.

Your eyes are blurred. You can hardly see, hardly see. Your eyes are wet and uncomfortable. Your eyes are strained. The strain is getting greater and greater, greater and greater. Your lids are heavy. Heavy as lead. Getting heavier and heavier, heavier and heavier. They're pushing down, down, down. Your lids seem weighted, weighted with lead, heavy as lead. Your eyes are blinking, closing, closing. You will feel drowsy and sleepy, drowsy and sleepy. I shall now begin counting. At each count you will feel yourself going down, down, down into a deep comfortable, deep restful sleep. Listen carefully. One, down, down, down. Two, three, four, more and more, more and more. Five, six, seven, you are sinking, sinking. Nine, ten, eleven, twelve, deeper and deeper, deeper and deeper. You are falling fast asleep.[1]

Once the person has entered into a trance, the hypnotist might have the person imagine him/herself in a familiar or comfortable situation: Imagine yourself at a point in your life where you felt very successful. Recall your last vacation and remember how you felt. Or, the hypnotherapist may utilize a post-hypnotic suggestion to encourage the person to handle a nagging problem in a more creative manner. The following is an example of how a hypnotist might help a person to lose weight:

> The next time you feel like overeating, you will find that you will have the internal resolve to take control of your eating habits. Think about all the compliments you will get from your friends and loved ones. Imagine how proud you will feel when you reach your goal weight and wear the kind of clothes you have dreamed about wearing. In your mind's eye, you can see yourself eating less and exercising more. You can see the trim and fit image you really want. Maybe you can see yourself in a particular outfit or suit. As you listen to my voice, maybe you feel yourself getting lighter. You may even imagine yourself feeling very light. Light as a feather. You may also get a sense of increased energy and stamina. Take a moment to experience what it's like to be full of energy and pep. You may even feel a little younger. Perhaps you can see yourself at a time in your life when your body was fit and trim. Maybe you feel a little like you did when you were in high school or college.

While in this relaxed state, the person is more receptive to the vivid and positive images suggested by the hypnotist. Moreover, the person is capable of experiencing feelings and images that he or she could not experience in a non-hypnotic state. If one analyzes what happens during direct hypnosis, the similaritties between this process and the advertising communication process become quite apparent.

The advertiser, like the hypnotist, is concerned with getting the person's undivided attention and encouraging the viewer or listener to focus on one idea or image. In addition, the advertiser, like the hypnotist, often makes use of images, music, and language that create a relaxed feeling on the audience and compel the target audience to view issues in a new or different manner. In addition, the advertiser, like the hypnotherapist, is apt to repeat key words in order to reinforce the importance of certain benefits, features, or product characteristics. Last, like the hypnotist, the advertiser frequently wants his/her audience to imagine themselves as being different than they have been in the past. They both want people to perceive situations, problems, solutions to problems, and themselves in a new or different way.

In the same way that an effective hypnotherapist can get people to think about themselves in a new manner, a commercial might also help people to think about a product or a problem in a different manner than they have in the past. (For example, a commercial for something as mundane as a pencil might encourage people to think of this item as "a portable word processor.")

INDIRECT HYPNOSIS

While there are many similarities between direct hypnosis and the advertising process, it is perhaps more important for the advertising practitioner, entrepreneur, or business person to understand the nature of what is often referred to as indirect hypnosis and how this persuasive tool can be integrated into advertisements. This form of hypnosis, sometimes called conversational hypnosis, has been used by religious leaders, politicians, teachers and others for years.

According to Moine and Lloyd (1990), the structure of indirect hypnosis was first described by Richard Bandler and John Grinder. These researchers studied Dr. Milton Erickson's work quite carefully. Dr. Erickson, an eminent psychiatrist and hypnotherapist, was able to induce hypnotic states in virtually every person he encountered. Moine and Lloyd point out that there are four essential steps involved in Erickson's conversational or indirect hypnosis. These steps are very similar to what copywriters and art directors do when they create an advertisement or commercial.

1. Hold and Fixate the Person's Attention

While traditional hypnosis relies on devices like a shiny object or a watch swinging from a chain, indirect hypnosis asks the person to concentrate on an event, an emotion, a belief, or a feeling. The hypnotist might ask the person to think about how he or she feels when in a specific situation. Similarly, the advertising practitioner often attempts to get his or her audience focused on a singular problem, point, feeling, attitude, or situation. This single-mindedness is often facilitated by the headline in a print advertisement, the initial visual in a television commercial, and the first sound in a radio spot.

2. Present Undeniably Truthful Ideas That Are Impossible to Disagree With

The second step of conversational hypnosis is to present ideas or perceptions that are impossible to disagree with. For instance, the hypnotherapist might remind a person that many people with the same affliction as the patient have been helped and had the same problem solved in a short period of time. Likewise, the advertiser can cite statistics about the success that others have had with a particular product. These ideas or perceptions help a patient to feel that the therapist understands his or her problem. In a similar manner, the presentation of these facts communicates to readers or listeners the feeling that the manufacturer, spokesperson, or marketer understands their situation, needs, wants, and desires.

In the same way that a therapist communicates the idea that he/she understands the patient's situation, the advertiser must let the target audience know that the company or product has the capacity to help people solve their problems. Communicating in this way helps to build trust between the hypnotist and the client in the same way that it helps to create a bond between the advertiser and the target audience.

3. Increase the Readiness to Respond and to Take Action

Once the facts have been communicated clearly and a good rapport has been established, the hypnotist and the advertiser must strengthen the person's desire and eagerness to act. In order to achieve this objective, it is frequently necessary to free the person from fixed mental habits. A hypnotist might intensify a person's need to respond by presenting the client with ideas that are acceptable, but quite unexpected. This puts the client in a position of "being between decisions." Once a person is in this teetering position, he or she often changes behavior or makes a decision in order to eliminate the anxiety and confusion the persons is apt to be experiencing.

According to Moine and Lloyd (1990), Erickson used this approach when he treated severely obese patients. These patients feared that their appetite and their weight were out of control. He would hypnotize them and suggest they intentionally gain weight, so they would learn that they could control their caloric intake and expenditure. Since this was the first time that many of these overweight people had been given permission to gain weight, they experienced the suggestion as a surprise. Consequently, once many of these patients gained the feeling of control that they previously felt they didn't have by intentionally gaining weight, it was usually quite easy for Erickson to point out to them that they could also lose weight. By surprising his patients with a new experience and by furnishing them with a new perspective, Erickson was able to influence these people to behave differently.

Like Erickson, copywriters and advertisers must frequently present some surprising information about their product in an unexpected manner in order to get people to view the product and their relationship to the product in a different light or in a new way.

4. Provide a Clear and Direct Course of Action

Once the advertiser or hypnotist has gotten the person's attention, built a climate of agreement by presenting undeniable truths, and increased the person's readiness to act, the person or audience must be guided in the appropriate direction. For the hypnotherapist, this might be a homework assignment for the patient. For the advertiser, it might be a free trial offer, an invitation to test-drive a car, or a reminder to call an 800 number. It should be quite apparent by now that advertisers, sometimes knowingly and sometimes unknowingly, utilize direct and indirect hypnosis in their sales messages. Furthermore, it should also be quite apparent that many advertisements and commercials can be strengthened by the use of a hypnotic framework. Integrating hypnotic techniques into advertising messages that appear in various media will be discussed later in this book.

At this point, you probably understand some of the connections between hypnosis and advertising. Again, I must reiterate that I do not for a moment think that every effective sales message places people in a trance. That would be absurd. I do, however, believe that it is very useful to think of some of your advertisements and commercials as being similar to the hypnotic process or to a hypnotic induction. Furthermore, as you will see in the next chapter, much of what I have told you about hypnosis will be very helpful when you need to develop copy and graphics for your sales messages.

At this point, in order to further clarify the way hypnotic techniques can be utilized in advertising, I would like to give you a few more illustrations of sales messages that rely on hypnotic principles and techniques.

SOME EXAMPLES OF HYPNOTIC
ADVERTISING MESSAGES

Many of the most successful advertising campaigns of all time rely on what may be thought of as hypnotic techniques. While I could probably write an entire book about advertisements and commercials that have hypnotic qualities to them, I will comment here on just a few that come to mind. My hope is that you, the entrepreneur, will get a sense of how you can utilize hypnotic messages to penetrate the media clutter and communicate more effectively with your target audience.

The Cowboy Who Sold Billions of Cigarettes

I am adamant when it comes to my anti-smoking attitudes and feelings. However, as an ad man, I have nothing but love and admiration for the infamous Marlboro Man. The powerful appeal of this character has been written about by many writers and advertising critics. Yet I believe that there is much the entrepreneur can learn about hypnotic advertising by analyzing the reasons for the

Marlboro Man's marketing power. It's hard not to love the cowboy if you're an American male. After all, he spends his time in some of the most beautiful scenery in the world. He is John Wayne, Henry Fonda, and Alan Ladd all rolled into one. He rides beautiful horses and is the quintessential rugged individualist.

Travel around the country and you will see a lot of men who seem to be imitating the Marlboro Man. In the casinos of Nevada and the truck stops throughout the western and southwestern United States, you can find hundreds of men who are dressed just like the Marlboro Man. Sure, the clothing is functional for people who do outdoor work, but this man's image and clothing communicate ideas and feelings that transcend practicality: they are hypnotic because they take us back to a time when there was no pollution. They remind us of all those Westerns in which the good and bad guys were easy to identify. There were no shades of grey and no complications. Life was pure and simple. And if you were a rugged, good-looking guy, you could have a great time. The Marlboro advertisements, billboards, and commercials create or suggest tales of the Old West in the minds of the people who are exposed to them. Interestingly, these tales of American cowboys are also as popular abroad as they are here.

Thousands of other commercials attempt to create tales, images, fables, or allegories. Calvin Klein's Obsession commercials recreate erotic fantasies.

John Caples, the famous copywriter wrote a classic ad with the headline "They Laughed When I Sat Down At The Piano, But When I Started To Play. . . ." that tells the story of a man who dazzles people at a party with his newfound musical talent. This ordinary fellow becomes a hero because he has taken music lessons through a correspondence course.

Many advertisements and commercials create heroes. The Man From Glad, The White Knight, The Man Who Wears The Star, and Mr. Clean are just a few of the heroes who have been associated with widely sold products and major corporations. Heroes have the power to captivate and mesmerize large numbers of people. Watch what happens during Old Timers Day at Yankee Stadium when Mickey Mantle or Joe DiMaggio shows up. Invariably, the crowd becomes overwhelmed with emotion. Heroes remove us from our everyday lives. They have a godlike power over us. I was recently at a meeting with a group of entrepreneurs who were trying to communicate to their audience the idea that their company was back in business after experiencing some financial reversals. Since they could not afford Bo Jackson, I suggested that we use a local athlete who had recently returned to action after a serious injury. Associating a pre-existing hero with a product or creating a new one is often a sure-fire way of getting your audience's undivided attention, creating a feeling or mood they will enjoy, and putting your company or product on the map.

SHOCK AND CONFUSE YOUR AUDIENCE

As I mentioned earlier in this chapter, the psychotherapist, like the politician or the salesman, must sometimes shock his or her audience in order to gain their attention and get them to perceive things in a new manner. Similarly, some advertisements and commercials shock the viewer or reader by creating an image or situation you could never find in reality. A striking visual or an old song in a new environment can help to fixate the audience's attention on the message and force them to ask, "What's going on here?" Watch television for a few hours and you will notice how many commercials are intended to momentarily confuse or startle viewers in order to keep them involved with the message.

Milton Erickson, the psychiatrist and hypnotherapist mentioned earlier in this book, was a master of the art of persuasion. Erickson used to get his patients' attention by using many of these kinds of techniques. Like creative directors and copywriters, he used surprise, shock, confusion, questions, puns, and humor to influence the way his patients felt about themselves and the world. These elements would sometimes be incorporated into tales Dr. Erickson used to tell to his patients during their psychotherapy sessions. Sidney Rosen, a psychiatrist who studied with Erickson, describes these tales in detail in his book *My Voice Will Go With You: The Teaching Tales of Milton H. Erickson* (1982). According to Rosen, most of these tales had a structure and plot and many had a surprise ending. The stories would usually build to a climax, followed by a feeling of relief or surprise. The following is a tale intended to encourage people to be optimistic and hopeful in spite of life's inevitable disappointments. This tale was taken from Dr. Rosen's book.

OATS

I spent one summer grubbing up brush on ten acres of land. My father plowed it that fall and replanted it, replowed it in the spring, and planted it into oats. And the oats grew very well and we hoped to get an excellent crop. Late that summer, on a Thursday evening, we went over to see how that crop was getting along, when we could harvest it. My father examined the individual oat stalks and said, "Boys, this is not going to be a bumper crop of thirty-three bushels per acre. It will be at least a hundred bushels per acre. And they will be ready to harvest next Monday."

And we were walking along happily thinking about a thousand bushels of oats and what it meant to us financially. It started to sprinkle. It rained all night Thursday, all day Friday, all night Friday, all day Saturday, all night Saturday, all day Sunday, and in the early morning on Monday the rain ceased. When we were finally able to wade through the water to that back field, the field was totally flat; there weren't any upright oats.

My father said, "I hope enough of the oats are ripe enough so that they will sprout. In that way we will have some green feed, for the cattle this fall–and next year is another year."

And that's really being oriented to the future, and very, very necessary in farming.[2]

Within the clinical milieu, these kinds of tales have several purposes. They are intended to get patients to relax and focus on a new way of viewing, thinking about, or experiencing a problem or issue that had been troubling them. These tales mesmerize many people and help them to view their difficulties in a different way than they are able to in their normal, conscious state. The tales also circumvent the conscious mind, which contains much of the person's self-doubt, sadness, and emotional clutter. Instead, they tap into the rich and powerful unconscious mind, which has the capacity to free many people and allow them to change.

Like most people, you have probably had the frustrating experience of using reason and logic with virtually no success when you have been trying to communicate with another person. Salesmen, advertising experts, and psychiatrists will tell you that people sometimes simply fail to respond to logic. Sometimes, a tale or a story can drive home a point or idea in a more effective manner than can a logical argument. Some hypnotherapists believe that the trance experience, which can be induced through traditional induction techniques or by the telling of a tale, enables people to perceive their universe in a different way and thus facilitates changes in their thoughts, feelings, beliefs, and actions. Facilitating new ways of looking at things is important for psychotherapists as well for advertisers, marketers, entrepreneurs, and communicators of all types.

Many of Erickson's tales were intended to relax people and help them to feel that they could develop new, more effective feelings, attitudes, and behaviors. In some ways, these tales resemble the fascinating and often inspiring bedtime stories that parents have recited for their children for hundreds of years. Rosen (1982) describes his own experiences with these tales in the following way:

> Erickson often used descriptions of earliest childhood development–learning to recognize one's own hand, learning to stand, to walk, and to talk–as a way of building a person's sense of his own process and growth. When he told me stories in which I was directed back to my earliest learnings, I was able–in the trance state–to reexperience the immense effort and frequent frustration involved in learning any new task or skill. At the same time, I was perfectly aware that I had learned these skills successfully. The implication was that I could learn to overcome other challenges in my present life.

Like Erickson's tales, many effective print advertisements try to capture the reader's attention and create a new awareness, experience, or knowledge in the reader's mind. Furthermore, many advertisements show people how they can approach old situations in a new, more effective manner. And this is precisely the kind of effect many of Erickson's tales had on his patients. These tales facilitated new learning that may not have been feasible by merely encouraging patients to develop a different or new way of looking at a problem or dilemma. It appears that the symbolic messages in these tales had a more powerful impact than a straightforward message from the therapist might have produced.

Erickson used a variety of these tales to help people reach their fullest potential. People suffering from a wide range of psychological and physical problems were frequently helped from hearing these tales. These tales were also used by Erickson to help athletes enhance their skills. Sometimes, before hearing the tales, people would be placed into a trance through a formal induction like the one described earlier in this chapter. In other instances, the tale itself would produce the trance.

Like these tales, many commercials and advertisements are intended to surprise or shock people so that they will attend to the message and feel, in some way, different than they did prior to noticing the advertisement. This "different feeling" can be induced by sound, images, colors, typography, and language. Likewise, a new way of thinking about something can be initiated by a clever graphic or design. The Transamerica Life Insurance pop-up advertisement generated a lot of visibility and public relations because it presented a three-dimensional message for a medium that almost always presents two-dimensional messages.

When an advertiser uses radio to get a message out, he or she may use a unique sound or a key word or phrase that may be repeated several times throughout the spot. (Isn't this very much like what the hypnotist does when he or she repeats key words over and over again?) If you are going to use radio or television in your campaign, you may want to use an announcer with a powerful voice that will get your audience's attention and have the capacity to induce a mild trance in listeners. Or, you may choose to use a song that instantly creates a distinct mood among listeners. Music can immediately change your audience's frame of mind and get them to focus on your message. Furthermore, music can get people to perceive your product and your company in a different way. Several years ago, a podiatrist asked me if I could come up with a unique idea for promoting his practice through a radio advertising campaign. I suggested he use the Beach Boys song "Take Good Care Of Your Feet." I felt that this tune would bring some levity to the field of podiatric medicine. In addition, if the right kind of informative copy was intermingled with this catchy, comical, and upbeat tune, it could help people to think of the podiatrist in a way they probably never had before.

REPETITION AND ITS ROLE IN HYPNOTIC ADVERTISING

Hearing the same slogan, jingle, or music can also help place consumers into a mild trance. How many times have you found yourself humming a jingle? Have you ever noticed how a jingle can change your mood? This kind of hypnotic repetition can help to reinforce sales messages. Similarly, seeing the same outdoor billboard every day while driving to and from work may have a hypnotic impact on some individuals. Furthermore, seeing a slew of messages on a highway for the same business or related business can help to induce a trance among drivers. When you approach Las Vegas or Atlantic City, for example, you are exposed to dozens of the same kinds of messages in a short period of time. My guess is that this kind of outdoor advertising helps to excite people about the gambling and other activities available to them in these cities. Furthermore, people who visit Las Vegas or Atlantic City are exposed to similar messages when they leave. Seeing this kind of advertising on your way home probably helps to plant the idea of returning to these gambling cities once again.

NOTES

1. Reprinted from *General Techniques of Hypnotism*, Andre M. Weitzenhoffer. New York: Grune & Stratton, 1957. Reprinted by permission of author.
2. Reprinted from *My Voice Will Go with You: The Teaching Tales of Milton H. Erickson*, edited by Sidney Rosen, by permission of W.W. Norton & Company, Inc. © 1982 by Sidney Rosen, MD.

Chapter 5

Words That Win Customers:
A Short Course in Copywriting

Now that you know a little about persuasion and hypnotic advertising and have a handle on your product, your customer, your competition, as well as the problem or problems you want your advertising to solve, you can start to think about your message, the story you want your advertising to tell, and the tone of your advertising.

HOW DO YOU START?

I have taught hundreds of people how to create sales messages. In fact, writing copy is probably one of my favorite parts of the advertising process. I love the simplicity and challenge of creating an advertisement, a commercial, a direct mail letter, or a brochure for a product or service. Like a lot of other people who work in advertising, I have had an interest in writing and creativity for some time. I wrote my first play at age seven. It was a kind of flip-flop of a television show that was quite popular when I was growing up–*The Beverly Hillbillies*. After watching this show for several weeks, it occurred to me that a series portraying city people who had been suddenly moved to a rural environment would probably be as entertaining and interesting as the Clampetts. As you may recall, *Green Acres* became a very popular program shortly after *The Beverly Hillbillies* became a big success. My elementary school teacher thought my play was very clever. She wrote a nice note home to my mother, telling her how talented I was and she encouraged me to write another play.

For me, writing is a lot of fun. If you are someone who likes to generate ideas and has the capacity to look at things in a new or somewhat unprecedented way, you may have the stuff it takes to write your own effective advertising. In addition, if you are someone who can detect interesting relationships or analogies between what you are selling and other attractive themes or ideas, you can probably generate some very interesting concepts for your advertising program.

If you can get these kinds of thoughts down on paper or on the screen of your word processor, you are well on your way to becoming a good copywriter. Remember, virtually all sales messages begin with a written idea that is subsequently produced in one form of advertising or another. Furthermore, if you can think visually, draw, and like to spend time working on a computer, these skills and interests can be put to good use when you have to create copy for your venture. In fact, with the right word-processing programs, graphics software, and laser printer, you can probably prepare many advertising materials on your own. On the other hand, if you don't like doing these kinds of activities, you may elect to farm out your advertising projects (as many businesses do).

Good copywriters can come from all walks of life. Salespeople frequently have the ability to create advertisements that reflect their selling skills and their knowledge of persuasion and consumer behavior. Artists tend to generate advertisements with interesting concepts with exciting and entertaining visuals. People with English backgrounds know how to choose the right words and tend to have the capacity to link selling ideas in a logical and eloquent manner. Social scientists often have a good sense of the importance of selecting the right appeals, and they often carefully consider the demographic and psychographic nature of the target audience. Accountants, lawyers, and engineers are skilled at identifying and delineating the key selling points in the copy they produce.

To some degree, the fact that people with diverse backgrounds and talents can create effective sales messages is proof of the idea that there is no perfect or simple recipe or formula for teaching or learning copywriting. This process is part art and part science. I tell students in my copywriting class that this course is an adventure in the worlds of business, writing, and creative ideas. We spend a lot of time learning how to solve business communication problems, how to be more creative, and how to sell and communicate more effectively. We look at hundreds of successful and unsuccessful sales messages and we write copy for dozens of different products, services, and businesses. Students also write public service announcements designed to solve social problems like crime, drug abuse, teen suicide, and teen pregnancy. When students finish the class, they know how to write effective copy and they understand what differentiates a potentially effective message from one that is likely to fail.

As I noted, while there is no perfect recipe for copywriting, I try to provide students with some guidelines, strategies, and techniques that will point them in the right direction. In this chapter, I will give you a few guidelines that should help you to improve your copywriting skills. However, I would encourage you to view these principles as a map for a journey that you must take on your own. My suggestions and ideas will get you on the right path. However, I have seen many people go about the copywriting process in a variety of different ways, and lots of them still manage to produce wonderful, powerful advertisements.

While every entrepreneur cannot learn to be an award-winning advertising genius, many can learn how to recognize and produce an effective message. Furthermore, it is usually the entrepreneur himself or herself who has the best sense about how to market and promote the company's product or service. While an advertising agency or consultant can offer valuable input, advice, and direction, it is unlikely that these external resources will ever know more about the entrepreneur's business than the entrepreneur does.

WHERE DO IDEAS FOR ADVERTISEMENTS COME FROM?

As I have mentioned in preceding chapters, a lot of ideas are born from knowledge of your product, your customer, your competition, and your industry. Perhaps you recall what a satisfied customer has said about your product or business. This quote may be able to be used in your copy in some way. If you can recall a specific but illustrative problem that your product or service has solved for your customers, you can sometimes base your message on this case history. A flashback to an enlightening conversation you had with your sales force or your marketing director can also be transformed into an interesting and effective message. These kinds of real-life interactions can often serve as the foundation for your advertising campaign.

In addition, as I mentioned in the second chapter, ideas for ads come from observing and studying other ads. Read publications in which your competitors advertise. Take a look at advertising journals and books on award-winning campaigns. Review advertisements and commercials from other fields, since these can also serve as sources of ideas for your advertising. Always be on the lookout for new and interesting ways of communicating your main selling idea.

While some ideas are likely to come to you in a rather logical and predictable way, many copywriters get inspirations in the middle of the night, while they drive in their cars, or while they lather up in the shower. I suggest you keep a pen and pad nearby so you don't lose or forget a good idea when one sneaks up on you. If you feel lost or stuck or are suffering from a severe case of writer's block when you sit down to create your copy, write a customer paragraph like the ones you read earlier in this manual. These paragraphs always give my students an abundance of material they can utilize in their advertisements. If you spend some time writing these essays (and then reading them carefully), you will probably discover many ideas for headlines, body copy, and slogans. When you go through your paragraph, underline words, phrases, or language that seem to fit well in your advertisement. Try to identify potential headlines, body copy, quotes, selling points, and slogans.

Make a List of Selling Points

Sometimes, it is useful to simply itemize your product's unique features and benefits before you attempt to write any copy. Make a list of at least ten reasons for using whatever it is you are promoting. Try to think in terms of benefits to the user, as opposed to features of the product. That is, you need to focus on what people will get from the features of the product. Be sure to state these benefits from the consumer's perspective, not from your company's viewpoint.

Once you have a list of your strongest selling points, rank the items according to the most compelling reason for purchasing your product or utilizing your service. The most compelling reason often becomes the headline of your advertisement or the central concept for your entire advertising campaign. Many business owners wrongly assume that there is nothing unique about their operation. However, if they carefully analyze their company, they almost invariably discover something that can set them apart from the competition. In some instances, the entrepreneur gets an idea for changing or improving his or her operation after engaging in this kind of internal evaluation. As a matter of fact, when I discuss these issues with clients, they frequently discover new and exciting directions in which to move their companies.

WHY BEGIN WITH PRINT ADVERTISEMENTS?

As you have probably noticed, I am spending a lot of time talking about writing print advertisements. This may seem odd to some of you since there are so many different media available to the 1990s entrepreneur. In fact, many students ask me why I spend so much of the term on print advertisements when there are so many other advertising media to select from.

There are several reasons for teaching copywriting in this manner. First, it is usually quite easy to transform a good print advertisement into an effective television commercial, radio spot, brochure, billboard, or direct mail letter. If you have an idea that is well-conceived and effectively executed, it is easily adapted to other media. Second, most sales messages tend to resemble print advertisement in their structure and organization. Third, most entrepreneurs will probably spend a large portion of their budgets on print media. Last, it is generally easier to start with print advertising, since you do not have the time and production constraints that typically accompany the development of commercials in the electronic media. Rest easy, though, I will talk about other forms of advertising in subsequent chapters.

The Components of the Print Advertisement

If you have followed my instructions so far, you should now have some rough ideas of what your advertisement may say and what it might look like. Most print advertisements include the following elements.

The Headline

As you probably know, the headline is the most important element of the print advertisement, according to numerous advertising experts. Books on copywriting usually devote a substantial amount of space to the writing of headlines. When I teach introductory copywriting classes, forty percent of the class time is spent on learning to create effective headlines.

As I alluded to earlier on, a good headline ought to compel members of the target audience to read the rest of the message. This objective can be achieved in a number of ways:

1. The headline can include a provocative question.
2. The headline can state an interesting fact about your product, your industry, the reader's problem, or a solution to that problem.
3. The headline can present a consumer benefit, promise, or offer that your competitors can't make.
4. The headline might encourage the reader to think about an issue in a way that they never have before.
5. Some effective headlines present news to the reader.
6. You may decide to identify and speak directly to your target audience in your headline (e.g., "Attention, Mercedes-Benz Owners").
7. A headline can be the first part of a riddle, joke, or humorous anecdote.
8. Some headlines relate specifically to the graphic or photo contained in the ad. That is, they raise a question about the visual component of the ad or include a quote from one of the people in the photograph or graphic of the advertisement.
9. The headline may identify an analogy or concept that will be of interest to your reader.
10. The headline might include a clever play on words or a double meaning. These kinds of headlines can hold readers' interest long enough to get them to read the subhead or the body copy to get more information.

11. Last but not least, the headline may induce the kinds of hypnotic states you have read about earlier in this book.

How long should headlines be? Clients and students frequently raise this question, and I always answer it in much the same way. I've seen powerful headlines that are one word, and I have seen other super headlines that are twelve to twenty words long. It all depends on how interesting, exciting, and captivating the lead line is. Write as much as you need to get the job done!

The Graphic, Photo, or Illustration

In most large advertising agencies, copywriters work in conjunction with artists. In theory, the artist is responsible for the visual aspect of the ad, while the writer is looked upon as the wordsmith. In reality, however, the artist is sometimes the one who comes up with language and the writer is the one who thinks up the idea for the picture. When two creative people work together, all kinds of interesting thoughts and solutions to advertising problems frequently arise. In an effective print advertisement, the art work and the copy must work together if the message is going to be effective.

Art directors have an enormous array of graphic tools and devices to select from when they design an advertisement. Look through any magazine and notice the different uses of photographs, drawings, typography, layouts, color, and computer graphics. Some advertisements tell stories; some display products. Others bombard the reader with lots of information. Some layouts emphasize words; others call attention to images. Some make comparisons; others present analogies. Many ads have no picture, but are extremely attractive because of the layout and typography incorporated into the advertisement.

In fact, computer graphics have greatly enhanced the visual tools that are at the disposal of art directors. Products can now be presented in ways never before possible. As I mentioned earlier, the computer also makes it possible for entrepreneurial companies to produce many of their promotional materials in-house.

The Subhead

The subhead performs a number of important functions in the sales message. For example, the subhead often expands on the idea introduced in the headline. The subhead also acts as the link between body copy and the headline. Similarly, it frequently connects the headline with the photo or graphic elements of the advertisement.

You can better understand the importance of the subhead if you think about the way a lot of people read advertisements. The headline or graphic gets people's attention; it is often the subhead or the first line of body copy that will determine if they read the rest of the copy. The subhead usually appears in italic type so it will stand out from the headline and the body copy.

The Body Copy

The body copy may be thought of as the "guts" of the advertisement. Here is where you tell your story in detail. Good copywriters will slave over the body copy the same way they do over headlines. Every word plays an important part in this form of marketing communication. Obviously, the body copy expands on the ideas presented in the headline and subhead line.

In the body copy, you may include additional facts, more reasons to read the rest of the advertisement, supplemental information about your company, your product or offer, or additional reasons to select your business instead of the business down the street. The body copy also tells the story that will change the way people feel about your company or reinforce certain feelings and ideas that they may already have.

The body copy is also the place where you present all of the key points that comprise your selling argument.

The Slogan

The slogan (or tag line, as it is sometimes called) is another important part of the print advertisement. Large companies can spend thousands of dollars and man-hours on developing an appropriate slogan. And in some instances, the slogan will be changed, updated, or modified when it becomes stale, when the company elects to change its direction, or adapt its mission statement.

The slogan serves a number of functions within an advertisement. First, it sums up the story that the ad tells to the reader. Second, it identifies and helps people recall the company's name and the company's purpose for being. Third, it helps to enhance the company's image in the mind of the target audience. A good slogan is catchy, succinct, simple, and to the point. It should never be a cliché, and it should never sound like a slogan used by one of your competitors.

The slogan ought to be something that can be utilized in all forms of advertising. When you pick one for your business, make sure it is suitable for every medium you may consider using in the future. Also, make sure it is general enough and flexible enough to allow your business to grow and expand in several directions.

The Logo

Large companies also invest a substantial amount of time and money in their logos. Within the context of a print advertisement, the logo does many of the same things the slogan does. In other words, it identifies the company that has placed the ad, enhances the company's image, helps to make the advertisement more attractive, and improves the recall and recognition of the message.

The design, color, and character of the logo should communicate something about the image and nature of the company or the business. Again, as with the slogan, don't use a design that resembles one your competitor uses. Create a logo that says something positive and unique about your firm. It is not uncommon to review a few dozen sketches until you discover the right symbol for your business. Figures 1, 2, and 3 illustrate logo designs.

GENERAL SUGGESTIONS ON COPYWRITING

New copywriters tend to make rather predictable mistakes. Here are a few guidelines to help you eliminate these typical errors from your sales messages:

FIGURE 1

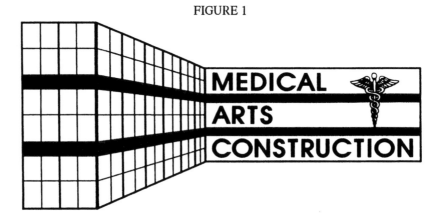

FIGURE 2

1. Don't be dull. If your message is boring, it won't get noticed and your advertising dollars will have been wasted.
2. Don't imitate your competitor. Although it is tempting to model your advertising after a program that is already successful, a copycat kind of strategy will almost always fail and come back to haunt you and your business. Furthermore, it will do little to build a recognizable and distinct image for your venture. In addition, you may risk a lawsuit if you closely imitate the advertising of a company in your industry.
3. Make sure you get your big idea in the headline. Don't ever bury your best sales argument in the body copy.
4. Don't write a headline that is too general. Make sure your headline is specific to your product, and be certain it makes a

promise that can be associated only with your company. Many of my students make the mistake of writing headlines and advertisements that can pertain to several industries or products. These non-specific headlines can cause your advertisement to be passed over.

5. Keep your language simple. You are not writing an essay to impress a college professor. You are trying to write a piece of sales communication. Keep it simple, straightforward, and to the point. Also, bear in mind that the English language has small words for big things. Words like love, war, Mom, home, and hope. Simple words like these communicate many emotions, thoughts, and images to your reader.

6. In most instances, you will want to write from your target audience's perspective. (See Figures 4 and 5.) Ads written from the company's perspective can sound boastful and may turn people off.

7. Your ad does not have to be clever or funny to be successful. (See Figure 6.) In fact, sometimes ads that are very entertaining fail to communicate effectively with the reader. On the other hand, if you can write copy that is informative, interesting, and entertaining, you can probably create some fantastic sales messages for your business.

8. Don't be reluctant to use the selling words that appear in advertisements all the time. You don't have to reinvent the wheel when it comes to words that sell. Use words other copywriters have used for years: new, now, you, your, yours, free, special, introducing, sale, announcing, opportunity, how to, act now, and bonus.

9. Demonstrate your product's benefit in an unusual, humorous, or provocative manner. For example, a carpet manufacturer placed one of their products on the streets of Manhattan prior to the start of the "Mother Of All Parades" that welcomed home the Persian Gulf troops. Thousands of people stomped on this carpet during the parade. This was an interesting and timely way to show the durability of this fabric. Similarly, Motorola developed an interesting way of demonstrating the durable nature of their cellular phones by producing a series of commercials showing children, dogs, and drivers abusing

the phones. In one of the spots, a driver smashes several car windows with the phone in an attempt to kill a bothersome bee that has flown into his car. Although these are examples of television commercials, you should, whenever possible, consider a novel way of demonstrating your product's assets and strengths in print advertisements as well.

10. Tell your story from a different perspective. This is a good technique for making your advertisements more interesting. Several years ago, one of my students wrote an advertisement for hot sauce. What was interesting about his message was that he wrote it as if the eggs were talking. The yolks of two sunny-side-up eggs comprised the face. "Put a lot of sauce on me today," the eggs told the eater. "It's kind of cold out, and I'd like to feel a little warmer. I can't wait to feel the sauce all over my face." This was a rather clever and humorous way of drawing attention to the product. It's also a good example of how telling a story from a different perspective can be an effective advertising tactic.

How Do You Know If Your Advertisement Will Work?

Every entrepreneur would like to have a crystal ball that would predict whether a planned advertising campaign was going to be effective or not. Unfortunately, while I can give you some general guidelines, there are no perfect formulas for success in this business. If there were, advertising agencies would never lose accounts and their clients would remain clients for life.

Nevertheless, there are a few barometers you can utilize to determine if your message seems to headed in the right direction. (By the way, you can use these formulas to evaluate any sales message, regardless of the medium in which it is to appear.) One of the quick tests I use to evaluate an advertisement is based on a model that has been around for quite some time. In fact, a gentleman in his sixties who attended one of my workshops told me that his college advertising professor taught the AIDA formula to him forty years ago. This formula is simple, comprehensive, and easy to remember,

FIGURE 3

especially if you're an opera lover. As some of you probably know, it is:

A = Attention

I = Interest

D = Desire

A = Action

FIGURES 4 and 5. These two advertisements communicate the idea that patients will be taken care of right away.

If You're Sick Or In Pain, A Park South Doctor Will Take Care of You Right Away.

IMMEDIATE CARE

You don't have to wait in a crowded hospital waiting room anymore.

Now you can see a private doctor and get quality, affordable medical care-7 Days A Week.

- Colds & Sore Throats
- Sprains & Strains
- Gynecological Exams
- Cuts
- Lung & Heart Problems

- Stomach Problems
- X-Rays
- Minor Emergencies
- Work/School Physicals
- High Blood Pressure & Diabetes

Call For An Appointment Or Just Walk In

PARK SOUTH MEDICAL & DENTAL ASSOCIATES

892-2200
Park South Medical & Dental
1545 Unionport Road
Parkchester, NY 10462

The Waiting Room.

You don't want to spend a lot of time there.-Especially when you're sick or in pain.
When you're not feeling well, a **Park South Doctor** will take care of you right away- **7 Days A Week.**
You don't need to wait in a crowded hospital waiting room anymore. We will take care of—

- Colds & Sore Throats
- Sprains & Strains
- Gynecological Exams
- Minor Emergencies
- High Blood Pressure & Diabetes
- Lung & Heart Problems
- Cuts & Bruises
- Work/School Physicals
- Stomach Problems
- X-Rays

**Now You Can See Your Own Private Physician
And Get Quality, Affordable Medical Care.**

PARK SOUTH MEDICAL & DENTAL ASSOCIATES

892-2200
Park South Medical & Dental
1545 Unionport Road, Parkchester, NY

FIGURE 6. The message in this ad promotes preventive dental care. This ad, along with the ads in Figures 4 and 5, generated many new patients and enhanced the image of this clinic.

You Don't Need A Toothache To See A Park South Dentist.

IMMEDIATE CARE

Lots of people wait until they are in pain to see a dentist.

At Park South Dental, we would like to see you and take good care of your teeth-before a problem begins.

Of course, if you have a toothache, we will get rid of the pain as quickly as possible.

And we'll show you how to keep your teeth healthy.

At Park South, you'll get quality, affordable care from a private dentist-**7 days a week.**

Call Us Now And Schedule Your Appointment.

PARK
SOUTH
MEDICAL & DENTAL
ASSOCIATES

892-2200
Park South Medical & Dental
1545 Unionport Road
Parkchester, NY 10462

In short, every advertisement or commercial you create must gain your audience's attention; develop an interest in the product, service, message, or offer; produce a desire for whatever is being sold; and compel people to act. If your message can accomplish these four objectives, your advertisement is probably on the right track. If you like, you can rate your sales message by assigning a twenty-five-point value to each aspect of this formula. If your advertisement scores low on a particular element, you ought to strengthen that part of the message.

The NICE Method

Some time ago, I was asked to be a judge in an advertising contest sponsored by the cellular phone industry. Before we began evaluating the advertisements, commercials, direct mail pieces, and brochures, each of the judges was asked to identify the criteria they looked for in an advertisement. Michael Denny, a copywriter who was on the panel, stated that he relies on the NICE method. In other words, the effective advertisement must be one or all of the following: Newsworthy, Interesting, Credible, and Entertaining.

The two other panelists and myself agreed on seven general criteria for analyzing each entry: attention getting; clarity of message; visual connection (between the message and its creative execution); salability; memorability; production quality; and overall presentation. All of these criteria were applied to print advertisements, direct mail pieces, television commercials, radio commercials, and sales promotion and multi-media campaigns (which included outdoor billboards).

The AIDA rule, the NICE formula, and the seven additional criteria provide useful guidelines to keep in mind when you are creating or evaluating your copy. If your advertising agency or consultant presents a sales message to you, you can rate it according to all or one of these barometers. Figures 7 and 8 present some samples of advertisements that produced good results for one of my clients.

Write Fifty Headlines or Create Fifty Images

Some of you will be inclined to think in words; others will think in pictures. I tend to start with words, but that's probably because I can't draw a straight line, even when I use a ruler. Generate whatever kind of idea you are most comfortable with first. The important thing at this point is to get the ideas from your brain onto your piece of paper or computer screen. Don't worry about whether your headlines are long or short, logical, crazy, or grammatically correct. Crank out phrases, ideas, promises, questions, quotes, analogies, sayings, statements, answers to questions, or slogans. Don't evaluate a thing now. Just let the ideas flow. Write down any thought that comes to mind no matter how irrelevant it might seem. Remember, some of the most creative and most successful campaigns are a result of someone thinking about something in a way that it was never thought of before. (See Figures 9, 10, 11, and 12.)

Do the same things with pictures. I encourage my students to free-associate during this phase of the creative process. Link ideas and words. Connect words with pictures. Write down everything

FIGURES 7 and 8. While these two advertisements could have been strengthened by photos of a couple in a wedding ceremony, the professional code in many states does not permit this kind of dramatization in advertising. Be aware of the codes and laws governing your industry before you advertise.

When you said these words, you thought your marriage would last forever.

But sometimes things change...

When your marriage is in trouble, you have to do all you can to protect yourself, your money, your home, and most of all—your children.

If your're thinking about a divorce or separation, you need a law firm that works closely with accountants to safeguard your financial assets and maximize your tax savings.

If you're thinking about getting out of your relationship and you need help, **now you can talk to a patient, caring and experienced attorney for free.**

Call Howard Pfeffer or Arnold Schancupp today and get your free copy of **Ten Things You Should Know About Divorce In New Jersey.**

SCHANCUPP & PFEFFER
Attorneys At Law
Edgewater Commons
81 Two Bridges Road, Fairfield, NJ 07006
(201) 227-9111

and anything that comes to mind when you think about your advertising problem and what you want your campaign to do. I find it helpful to draw lines and arrows connecting thoughts, pictures, or words that seem particularly relevant. If you've done the preliminary thinking and research I described earlier, you will probably be amazed at how much work your unconscious mind has already done in an effort to solve your advertising problem.

Sometimes, you will get lucky and the first picture or headline

"Your Home Is Your Castle"

Protect it.

Your home is probably the most valuable thing you will own in your life.

If you're thinking of buying or selling your home, the law firm of Schancupp & Pfeffer will protect your investment.

Arnold Schancupp and Howard Pfeffer have over 36 years of experience in real estate transactions. **They will see to it that you close on your property on time.**

Schancupp & Pfeffer will prepare or review your contract carefully. They will read all the fine print and make sure your interests are well-protected.

So, if you're buying or selling any real estate, call Schancupp & Pfeffer. They'll **return your phone calls promptly.**

Ask for your free copy of **9 Things You Should Know About Buying or Selling Real Estate in New Jersey.**

SCHANCUPP & PFEFFER
Attorneys At Law
Edgewater Commons
81 Two Bridges Road, Fairfield, NJ 07006
(201) 227-9111

you come up with will be the one you fly with. Other times, you will need to write down dozens of possibilities before you find the winner.

However, do not approach your search for the best headline in a rigid manner. That is, you may get in the way of the creative process by trying to settle on one headline or idea. Some of you will find it is more productive to choose three or four ideas you really like and then write some body copy for each of these favorites. You may even elect to use three different ideas in your campaign as opposed to one.

FIGURE 9. This is a promotional piece for my advertising services that I sent to presidents of a number of advertising agencies.

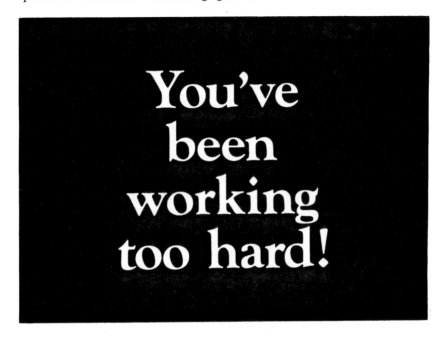

Running a small or medium size ad agency can be overwhelming at times. Long hours, client demands, personnel problems and the frantic pace of the industry can affect even a well-seasoned advertising executive.

Now you have an opportunity to reduce your work load and run your agency more efficiently. You have the chance to recruit an experienced, energetic and well-educated advertising professional who has the capacity to wear a number of different hats in your agency.

If you're looking for someone who can develop fresh concepts, communicate with clients, solicit new business and implement cost effective advertising campaigns, you ought to contact Jay Granat.

Mr. Granat has developed profitable campaigns for a wide range of products and services. He understands the importance of pragmatic product research, careful positioning, and communicating the products' unique selling points. Granat is familiar with direct mail, mail order, print campaigns as well as public relations techniques. He is a generalist who has worked as a copywriter, account executive and advertising consultant.

To obtain additional information about this multi-talented person call (201) 224-4680

You'll be on your way to reducing your work load, simplifying your life and increasing your agency's profits.

FIGURE 10. This advertisement targets car owners concerned about insurance laws. It informs about the dangers of these new laws and highlights this law firm's expertise in automobile accident cases. The firm received many requests for additional information from this full-page advertisement.

Don't Start Your Car

Until You Read This Important Message.

If you drive a car in New Jersey, you may be paying a lot of money for auto insurance without getting the protection you need.

To make sure that you and your family are fully protected in case of an auto accident, choose NO THRESHOLD when you renew your car insurance policy.

To protect your right to sue any driver who harms you or your loved ones, you must tell your car insurance agent you want a NO THRESHOLD policy.

Imagine being injured by a drunk driver and not being allowed to sue for damages. It just doesn't make sense for you to leave yourself unprotected.

Even if you have renewed your policy, you ought to call your auto insurance agent today, and say that you want to change to a NO THRESHOLD policy—NOW.

Sure, this added protection will cost a few dollars more. But if you don't have NO THRESHOLD coverage, you may give up your right to claim money from drivers who harm you.

Because we are one of the largest and oldest personal injury law firms with 10 offices in New Jersey, we feel it is our responsibility to keep you informed about laws which affect you.

So, if you have any questions about your rights or how to get a NO THRESHOLD policy, call us today toll free at 1-800-TEAM LAW for your free legal consultation.

Send us this coupon today and we will mail you free information that tells you how to get the insurance you need and protect your right to sue for a cash award.

Shevick, Ravich, Koster, Tobin, Oleckna & Reitman, P.C.

Call 1-800

TEAM-LAW

for injured people

☑ Yes, I want to protect my family, my right to sue and my right to collect money.

Please send me the information to get a NO THRESHOLD car insurance policy:

Name _____

Address _____ Apt. ____

City: _____ State: _____ Zip _____

Shevick, Ravich, Koster, Tobin, Oleckna & Reitman, P.C., 1743 St. Georges Avenue, Rahway, NJ 07065.

FIGURE 11. This business-to-business advertisement was directed toward people who treat addicts. This message focuses on the frustration which practitioners experience when working with this population.

You Don't Have To Be Frustrated By Cocaine And Crack Addicts Anymore.

Dr. Arnold M. Washton

Executive Director
The Washton Institute
4 Park Avenue
New York, New York 10016
(212) 213-4900

Now there are methods to help you treat these patients successfully.

Dr. Arnold M. Washton, internationally-known expert on cocaine addiction and author of Cocaine Addiction: Treatment, Recovery and Relapse Presention, will come to your facility and show you how to evaluate, treat and prevent relapses with cocaine and crack addicts.

Dr. Washton will show you and your staff HOW TO –

- evaluate and screen new patients • prevent early dropouts • treat sexually addicted patients
- manage difficult, unmotivated patients • help patients handle cravings and urges
- effectively use inpatient, outpatient and aftercare programs • prevent relapse
- use dozens of effective skills, strategies and techniques

If you want to treat your patients more effectively and need help, call Dr. Washton at (212) 213-4900.

Or complete the coupon on the back and send for more information.

FIGURE 12. This ad ran in many newspapers and produced many cases. Similar ads ran in the Yellow Pages and on the interiors of buses.

INJURED?

Now You Can Get
FREE LEGAL ADVICE
From a Team of Experienced Attorneys.

If you, or a loved one has been injured, you may deserve a large cash award.

After a free, confidential interview, we will tell you how to protect your legal rights!

If we accept your case, we'll stand by you from beginning to end.

If you've been hurt in a car accident, on the job, by an unsafe product or by a doctor's mistake, you owe it to yourself to contact one of the largest and oldest personal injury law firms in New Jersey.

There are never any legal fees unless we collect money for you. There may be costs in some cases which are payable at the conclusion.

Our fourteen attorneys, para-legals, research staff and secretaries provide courteous, professional and efficient services at our three convenient locations.

We'll even provide free transportation to our offices.

Shevick • Ravich
Koster • Tobin • Oleckna & Reitman
A Professional Corporation

"In Case Of Injury,
We're The Legal Team You Can Depend On."

Call today for your free consultation!

1743 St. George Avenue	60 Evergreen Place	1 S. New York Avenue
RAHWAY	EAST ORANGE	ATLANTIC CITY
(201) 388-5454	(201) 672-6551	(609) 344-7158

WHAT SHOULD YOU DO IF YOU
JUST CAN'T COME UP
WITH ANY GOOD IDEAS?

Periodically, every writer comes down with a case of writer's block. There are times when you will scratch your head, pound your fist against your desk, pace around your office, stare out the window, look at the ceiling, and still draw a blank. If this happens, there are a number of things you can do. First, you can walk away from the problem and let your unconscious mind do some work for you. Sometimes, engaging in a unrelated activity is all you need to do to get your creative juices flowing. I get ideas in all sorts of places: while showering, while driving in my car, after swimming, after playing tennis, while I watch the evening news, or when I read the Sunday paper. Personally, I find that the morning is when I usually do my best thinking. Perhaps it is because my unconscious mind has been working all night on the idea. In fact, when I wake up, I often find that I have a full head of steam and am totally energized and raring to go when my fingers hit the keyboard. My wife is amazed at how many advertisements I have created between 6 a.m. and 8 a.m. In addition, I find that if I leave off my writing in the middle of a sentence or a thought before going to bed, I wake up with an abundance of information that falls into place perfectly. It is almost miraculous how well this technique works for me. Try it and see if it works for you.

I like to write at a word processor, and I usually wear one of my twenty baseball hats when I sit down to create an advertisement or commercial. A friend of mine who is a copywriter in a large agency prefers to write with a large pad and a magic marker. Creative people tend to have a lot of idiosyncracies surrounding their approach to the creative process. If you visit the creative department of a large advertising agency, you will see the signs of the various people's creative work habits. Some like to write lying down. Others paste ideas all over their offices. Some play darts until they are inspired by the right thought. Others stare out the window while they search for the right adjective, headline, concept, or visual. After you work at writing copy for a while, you will also start to know which kinds of stimuli, cues, and routines get your creative juices flowing.

Sometimes, I like to play rock music while I write. Other times, I like complete silence and solitude. I enjoy writing and find that I can spend hours at the word processor without getting bored. In fact, sometimes, I lose complete track of time when I get involved with this kind of creative endeavor.

If I do get stuck, though, I sometimes use self-hypnosis to unlock my creativity. You may find this to be very helpful too. I have taught many of my copywriting students how to use self-hypnosis, and I have been amazed with the results. Many students who seem to be very uncreative begin to write some terrific advertisements when they unlock their creative instincts with hypnotic techniques. Read on and give it a try. You may also find this exercise useful for managing the stress that is a by-product of running your own venture. You may also find self-hypnosis to be quite helpful when you are searching for the best solution to a business problem.

SELF-HYPNOSIS FOR COPYWRITERS AND CREATIVE ENTREPRENEURS

In the previous chapter, I explained how hypnotic techniques can be used to activate the subconscious mind. The subconscious contains a lot of valuable information for the writer and/or the creative entrepreneur. For instance, there may be an experience somewhere in your subconscious mind that you can utilize in an advertisement or a commercial. Perhaps there is a memory, an image, or a tune that can be linked to a product or service you are promoting in a radio or television commercial. If you learn how to use self-hypnosis, you can often tap these inner resources and utilize them to solve a range of advertising and business problems. There are many ways in which you can place yourself into a hypnotic trance. Basically, you utilize many of the same techniques that the hypnotherapist utilizes when he/she is working with a subject.

When people first learn about self-hypnosis, they sometimes have concerns about not waking up from the trance. You need not worry about this. You will come out of the trance when you are ready to. Self-hypnosis is not so different from meditation and from what Benson (1978) has called the "relaxation response." That is, you might think of self-hypnosis as simply a way of creating a relaxed state for oneself. Le Cron (1971) describes a simple self-induction technique that is a good way to relax and activate your subconscious mind if you so desire. Learning how to be relaxed is very important when you are engaged in a creative task or when you are trying to solve a complex problem. In fact, it is sometimes one's anxiety or nervousness that blocks the flow of creative ideas. Once you get uptight about not being able to come up with a good idea, it usually gets harder for you to generate any creativity. In a relaxed state, however, creative ideas often flourish. As a matter of fact, when a hypnotherapist awakens a person from a trance, the subject often reports an image or insight that he or she was totally unaware of prior to going into the trance.

There are hundreds of methods for inducing a trance in oneself. Dr. Le Cron has outlined a standard method in his book *The Complete Guide To Hypnosis*. His instructions for self-hypnosis appear below. If you like, you can record this technique and use it whenever you like. You will probably find that the more you practice self-hypnosis, the more quickly and easily it will be for you to move into a trance. In addition, you will probably achieve a deeper trance as you start to use hypnosis on a regular basis.

* * *

According to Dr. Le Cron you should first make yourself comfortable, being sure your clothing is loose. It makes no difference whether you sit up or lie down, as long as you are in a comfortable position. Fix your gaze on something. While you watch it, let your eyes go out of focus if you can. Now take a deep breath. That helps you relax. The more you relax, the easier it is for you to slip into hypnosis. Soon, you will find you are more relaxed than you probably ever have been before. Just relax and let go. Soon your eyelids will begin to feel rather heavy. As you continue to look at the object you've selected, the eyelids will get heavier and heavier, heavier and heavier. Probably you will begin to blink a bit. There may be a slight watering of your eyes as the eye muscles relax more and more. The lids are getting heavier and heavier. Let them wink if they seem to want to wink. Let them close whenever they want to close. The lids are relaxing more and more, which is why they feel so heavy and want to wink. Soon they will want to close. The lids are relaxing more and more. Soon they will want to close. Let them close whenever you want to. They are so heavy. Getting still heavier. It's even hard to keep them open.

Take another deep breath now. Let your eyes close if they are not already closed. In a moment, you may find that you need to swallow. Swallow whenever you feel the need. Probably you are developing a listless, drowsy feeling. Drowsy and rather sleepy. Very drowsy, and you feel more and more drowsy as you relax still more. You can relax more now. Begin with your right leg. Make all the muscles taut. Wiggle the toes, stretch the muscles in your calf, and upper leg by moving your foot. Then let the muscles loosen up and go limp from your toes right up to your hip. Now do the same with your left leg, tightening all the muscles, then letting them go loose. Relax the whole leg from the toes to the hip.

Your body can relax more now. Let your stomach and abdominal muscles loosen. Then your chest and breathing muscles. The muscles of your back can loosen and be limp. Let them loosen completely. Now your shoulders and the neck muscles. Often we have tension in that area. Feel the tension going out of those muscles as they loosen. And now make your right arm stiff and rigid, then let it go completely relaxed. Let all the muscles go slack from your shoulder right down to your fingertips. Your arm will relax completely. In the same way, relax your left arm. Even your facial muscles will relax. Notice how comfortable you feel. All tension is leaving you, draining away. You are so very comfortable and drowsy now.

You will listen attentively to what is being said. If there are outside noises, you need pay no attention to them. They go in one ear and out the other. They are unimportant. Listen only to my voice.

Often there is a flickering of the eyelids when you are in hypnosis. It is one of the signs of hypnosis. Sometimes they do not flicker even if you are in hypnosis. If yours do, they will soon relax and stop fluttering as you sink deeper and deeper. Take still another deep breath and let yourself go completely. Enjoy the dreamy, drowsy feeling. Hypnosis is not sleep, for you are always fully aware. But you will feel so very drowsy. Such a comfortable, pleasant listlessness is creeping over you more and more as you relax so completely. Perhaps your whole body feels heavy, particularly your arms and legs.

Notice that your breathing has changed. You are breathing more from the bottom of your lungs–abdominal breathing–and you are breathing more slowly. Notice the feeling of comfort and well-being [that] has come over you. Give way to the listless drowsiness. Everyone enjoys being in hypnosis. It is so comfortable and pleasant. Your whole body is relaxed, and tensions seem to drain away.

Now you can go still deeper into this pleasant state. Let go; go deeper and deeper with each breath. Deeper and deeper. The deeper you go, the more comfortable and pleasant it seems. Now imagine that you are standing at the top of an escalator. See the steps moving down in front of you and see the railings. If you do not like to ride escalators, imagine a staircase instead. I will count backwards from ten to zero. If you are using the escalator, step on it as I begin to count, standing with your hand on the railing. Or if you use the staircase, start walking slowly down it as I count. You are all alone. It is your private escalator. When we reach zero, imagine you have reached the bottom and step off. Ten–and you step on. Each count will take you deeper and deeper. Nine (slowly), eight, seven, six. You are going deeper and deeper. Five, four, three, still deeper. Two, one, and zero. Now, step off the escalator or staircase. You can continue to go deeper with each breath you take.

Your arms and legs may feel quite heavy by now. They are so completely relaxed. But one of your arms is going to begin to lose any feeling of heaviness and will grow lighter and lighter. It's as if all the weight were draining out of it. It may be your right arm, or it may be the left. Let's see which one it will be. Soon, the one [that] is getting lighter will start to lift from its position. It's getting lighter and lighter. You may feel the fingers of the hand beginning to move a little, or the whole hand may lift. The hand will start to lift, to float up towards your face, but of its own accord, without conscious effort. It goes up by itself. The hand and arm are becoming still lighter. Lighter and lighter. The hand is beginning to float up. Up toward your face. The arm starts to bend at the elbow and lift.

It might be interesting to think of some part of your face where you want the fingers to touch when they reach your face. It could be your forehead, your ear, your chin–any part. But your subconscious mind will see that the fingers touch some different part of your face from the one you selected. Where will it touch? It is lifting higher and higher still. It is as light as a feather. Lifting. It can move a bit faster now. If it has not yet started, lift it a few inches to give it a start and it then will continue to move up of its own accord.

Your hand is lifting higher and higher. As it goes up, you can go still deeper. The higher your hand goes, the deeper you will go. The deeper you go, the higher your hand will lift. Soon the fingers will be making a contact, touching your face at some different place from the one you consciously selected. [They are] reaching out now to touch your face. The wrist [is] turning. The hand goes still higher. If your hand has not already touched, it will continue to rise while we speak of other things, continuing to go up until you feel it touch your face. Then the arm will go down to some comfortable position. If it has touched, you may lower it.

Let yourself go still deeper now. How comfortable you are. Drift still deeper and enjoy it. Deeper and deeper. You wish to learn self-hypnosis. As a matter of fact, all hypnosis is really self-hypnosis. The operator is only a guide; the subject is the one who does it. You can quickly learn to be able to hypnotize yourself, just as you have spontaneously slipped into hypnosis many times.

To learn self-hypnosis, you will have a formula to follow, certain things to do that will cause you to go into hypnosis. First, select some key word or phrase that will be the signal for you to slip into hypnosis when you think or say the word. But it will be effective only when you intentionally say it and wish to be in hypnosis. It will have no effect except when you use it for that purpose. A good phrase is "relax now," but select any word or phrase that you prefer to use.

To hypnotize yourself, take any comfortable position.You need not speak aloud, merely think the suggestions you will give yourself. Fix your gaze on something. Gaze at it intently for a moment or two (no more than three or four). Let your eyes go out of focus as you do so. Suggest to yourself that your eyelids are becoming heavier and heavier. Then let them close and say to yourself, Now I'm going into hypnosis. Take two or three deep breaths. Then repeat your key word or phrase three times, very slowly. As you repeat it, you'll be drifting into hypnosis.

You will want to go as deeply as possible. When you have repeated your key, take another deep breath and suggest, Now I'm going deeper. Use the imaginary escalator or staircase, while you yourself count backwards from ten to zero, including the zero. As you do this, you will sink deeper. Some people find it hard to visualize. If that is true with you, just counting backwards will take you deeper. Each time you use the backward count, it will cause you to go deeper.

The first four times you practice inducing self-hypnosis, go down another level while you count again. Each time it will take you deeper. With practice, you will then need to do this only once. After you've practiced self-induction four times, or even less if you are very successful, you can begin using it.

When you are ready to awaken from self-hypnosis, all you need do is give yourself the suggestion, Now I'm going to wake up. Then count slowly to three. You will then be wide awake. You will always awaken feeling relaxed, refreshed, and clear-headed. If at any time when you are in hypnosis there should be any reason for you to awaken at once, you will awaken instantly. If the phone rings, you should answer it. If there is a real danger such as a fire, you will awaken instantly and be completely alert. This would happen without this suggestion, for your subconscious mind would awaken you if there was danger of any kind.

When you have practiced four times, or if you are having good results sooner, you will be ready to open your eyes and stay in hypnosis. There are times and conditions where you may wish to have your eyes open. Opening your eyes need not cause you to awaken. Instead, as you open your eyes, you can slip even deeper into hypnosis. You can open your eyes and remain deeply in hypnosis. Your vision will be no different. At each playing of this recording, or if you hear these words spoken to you, you will be able to go deeper into hypnosis until you have learned it well.

Now I will count to three and you will then be completely awake and alert. Wide awake. One. You are beginning to awaken. Two. You are almost awake now. Three. Now you are wide awake and normal in every way. You feel wonderful. You are wide awake now.

And hasn't this been a pleasant experience? Now you will be able to hypnotize yourself at any time.

* * *

Milton Erickson, the famous psychiatrist and hypnotherapist whom I wrote about in the last chapter, could induce a trance through what he called "indirect hypnosis." If you are not comfortable with the structured and formal approach outlined above, you can place yourself in a trance by simply relaxing and shifting your focus to a particular event or memory, or by considering some of your important, successful life experiences. This trance may help you solve a wide range of advertising or business problems by simply relaxing you, or by placing you at a point in time in your life when you felt very successful. Maybe you passed a difficult exam. Perhaps you mastered a difficult athletic task. Maybe you solved a challenging mathematical problem. Or you might remember a time when a solution to a problem came to you when you least expected it. You know what that feels like. Out of the blue, you discovered the answer to a dilemma. Maybe you realized where you left the keys you had been searching for for several days. Maybe you recall a time when you woke up in the middle of a night with a very clear solution to a bothersome interpersonal conflict.

Remember, there is a tremendous amount of creative power and information in your subconscious mind. You can access this information by using a formal method of induction like Le Cron's, or by simply altering your mood and changing the way you traditionally problem-solve. If you can learn how to tap into it, you can use your unconscious to better manage a multitude of situations.

Sometimes, by recalling instances when you have achieved something, created something, or felt successful, powerful, and proud of yourself, you can bring these same feelings and resources and use them to solve current problems. In time, you may be able to turn over many of your creative (and perhaps some of your personal) problems to your unconscious mind. Many creative people know they will develop the right solution simply by trusting their unconscious mind. They say things like, "I know the right headline will come to me. I can feel it. If I get out of the office for a few hours, I'm certain I'll come back with a good idea."

According to O'Hanlon and Hexum (1990), Milton Erickson was counseling an artist in his thirties who complained that he had been trying for some years to paint a circus picture and had not even succeeded in sketching one out. Erickson gave him post-hypnotic suggestions regarding the painting of the picture. The artist called Erickson after completing the picture very quickly; amazingly, he had no conscious memory of having painted it. During the trance, however, he could see himself painting the picture and could recall that he, as well as some art judges, was satisfied with the quality of the work. Apparently, various aspects of the picture represented significant people in his life. And interestingly, after getting un-blocked and painting the picture, the man completed therapy and resolved the emotional problems he was seeking treatment for.

This anecdote is one of many that illustrate the way hypnosis can be utilized by creative people. Like Erickson, some of his disciples use tales as hypnotic devices to unlock creative solutions to a wide array of problems. Sidney Rosen, another psychiatrist and hypno-therapist whom I discussed earlier, believes there are several tales that can activate the unconscious mind and inspire creativity. These tales are reprinted from Dr. Rosen's book *My Voice Will Go With You*.

Bolo Tie

All our life, we learn to place limits on so many things. I [Erickson] can think of Bill Folsey, a KOOL-TV newsman. On a trip to Chicago he went to a restaurant, where the head-waiter informed him that he would have to wear a tie–and not that bolo tie that Bill was wearing. Bill asked the headwaiter, "What did you pay for your tie?"

The waiter said, very proudly, "Twenty-five dollars."And Bill said, "My tie cost two hundred dollars."

The waiter didn't know what to think. And Bill Folsey walked into the restaurant and took a seat where he *chose* to sit–while the waiter tried to give that some thought. That odd-looking thing that Bill Folsey had on! A two-hundred-dollar tie! While his was only a twenty-five-dollar one.

So have a dream. And, every time you dream, you have the right and the privilege of re-dreaming that dream, with another cast of characters. And, in that way you can discover many things you've been trained not to know. Your teachers, a long time ago, told you, "Look at me when you are speaking to me. Look at me when I'm speaking to you." And you learned, "Don't do this, don't do that. Wear the right clothes, the right shoes. Tie your shoestrings right." So much of our learning is based upon limited instructions that bar us from our own development of our understanding–and we get into patterns of being limited.

I taught my sons how to hoe a potato patch–by making designs. And all the time they are making designs with their hoes and hoeing the potato patch, they are wondering what their design will be. So, my sons learned to hoe a potato patch hoeing triangles, and more and more triangles, and, on their own they discovered that they could hoe circles and numbers, and letters.

And it is wonderful, to have a night's sleep, a sound and restful sleep and not find out until next week that you have dreamt that night. You didn't know about that dream–until a week later.[1]

According to Dr. Rosen:

The comments that Erickson made after the tale of the tie might seem to be irrelevant. Actually, they are his way of repeating and driving home the main points in his tale. The point is that we are limited in our patterns of understanding action. ("Wear the right clothes. . . . So much of our learning is based upon limited instructions.") The second point is that we can replace our limited, and limiting, instructions with new patterns–of our own devising ("circles and numbers, and letters"). Finally, Erickson frames his comments with the suggestion that the listener should discover new patterns in a dream. He should trust his unconscious mind to devise novel ways of overcoming habitual limitations.

I spoke with Dr. Rosen while I was writing this book, and he told me that the following short tale could also be very helpful in unlocking creativity and for motivating writers, entrepreneurs, and other creative people.

The Tarahumara Indians

The Tarahumara Indians of southwestern Chihuahua are the ones who can run a hundred miles–their blood pressures don't go up and their heartbeats don't change. Some entrepreneur took some hundred-mile runners to the Olympics (1928, Amsterdam). They didn't even place, because they thought twenty-five miles was when you warmed up! It hadn't been explained to them that their run was twenty-five miles long.

Rosen notes, "I sometimes think about that story when I am having difficulty getting into a task, when I am writing, repairing something around the house, frustrated by difficulties, or literally breathless from jogging. The phrase will come into my head–'I am just warming up now.' I usually find more energy available after this."

Recently, I told this tale to my tennis partner during a long, tough, and highly competitive doubles match. My partner was complaining of fatigue late in the third set. After I told her the story about the Indians, she seemed to get her second wind. She went on to play brilliantly and we won the match in a tiebreaker.

I hope that these tales and the self-hypnosis techniques described in this book will unlock your creative energies if you should encounter a case of writer's block or if you feel too tired to forge ahead with a creative endeavor.

NOTE

1. Reprinted from *My Voice Will Go with You: The Teaching Tales of Milton H. Erickson*, edited by Sidney Rosen, by permission of W.W. Norton & Company, Inc. © 1982 by Sidney Rosen, MD.

Chapter 6

Testing: A Scientific Approach to Advertising

There are whole books written on advertising research and testing. What I want to do in this chapter, however, is to teach you a few useful testing procedures and also present some examples of how I have used testing when developing campaigns for my clients and for my own entrepreneurial ventures.

GO STRAIGHT TO THE HORSE'S MOUTH

While you can get some valuable information from showing your ideas to staff members, friends, and colleagues, it is best to show the advertisement to potential customers or clients in order to obtain really meaningful feedback. Large advertising agencies and corporations do this kind of testing all the time in focus groups. When you show people your sales messages during the testing phase, pay close attention to their body language and their nonverbal cues when they react to your advertisement. In most instances, you want people to react with a smile, a nodding of their head, or some expression of enthusiasm. If they don't respond with interest, curiosity, or some positive emotion, your advertisement is probably flat, dull, and too weak to effectively promote your business.

When I teach copywriting courses, I frequently have participants present their advertisements to the class. If the majority of the class does not respond in a positive manner to the message, something is wrong. Maybe your headline is weak. It might be that the visual you have selected is inappropriate. It is possible that something that you thought was very clever just isn't. Maybe your message looks too much like other messages for similar products. People may even interpret your advertisement in an entirely different manner than you would have expected them to. Ask your test audience specific questions about what they like and what they do not. Ask them for suggestions on how the ad can be improved or strengthened. Ask them for suggestions about more effective headlines, graphics, copy, and design.

You may find it valuable to get feedback on four or five different advertisements for the same product or service. This will allow you to get a sense of which messages are on the right track and which are on the wrong track and why. You can use this information to decide which elements ought to be included, modified or eliminated. You can use this kind of testing for virtually every kind of sales message you create for your venture: brochures, television/radio commercials, direct mail letters, etc.

Since many of the campaigns I have worked on have been direct response programs, I am a firm believer in pragmatic testing of copy. I have tested numerous ads and commercials before rolling out full-scale advertising campaigns. Advertisers can learn a great deal, and increase their profits, if they utilize some basic testing techniques when they execute their communication programs. An example of one of my experiences with testing should give you an indication of the importance and value of approaching advertising in a scientific manner.

EXPANDING A CONSTRUCTION BUSINESS DURING A RECESSION

Some time ago, while the building industry was in the midst of a rather severe recession, I received a phone call from one of the owners of a family construction business. During our initial conversation, he explained that his business had dropped off significantly, and he was wondering if advertising could be helpful. We spent a few hours discussing the nature of the problems plaguing the construction business as well as his company's areas of expertise. Fortunately, his family had done some construction work in the medical and health care fields. Since this industry tends to be recession-proof, we thought it would be a good idea to target physicians who were in need of the services of a construction company.

The client told me that another team of advertising consultants had suggested direct mail as a way of reaching this group. While I didn't think this was a bad idea, I knew that a direct response campaign would cost about ten thousand dollars if it was done correctly. While direct mail is a highly cost-effective medium, there are a lot of front-end expenses (printing, postage, graphic design costs, and paper) that make the initial mailing quite expensive. Furthermore, my client wanted to reach doctors who were expanding their practice, moving offices, buying medical buildings, or opening an additional office. I felt that a mailing list that segmented these kinds of physicians would be very hard to locate. While we could easily rent a list of physicians from any number of list brokers, I believed there would be a lot of waste in this kind of list. That is, a lot of doctors would simply not be in need of my client's services at the time of the mailing. In short, I felt that the total cost of preparing the mail piece would be a bit too costly for this client at this particular time.

When I start to work with clients who have a small budget, it is helpful to them if we can start to generate some sales leads without spending a lot of money. Once clients get some feedback from the advertising, they feel encouraged and more secure about moving into a more expensive and comprehensive advertising campaign. I felt that we could generate some leads and some business without going through the time and expense involved in launching a direct mail program. (Besides the front-end costs, it can take several months to develop an effective direct mail package that includes a letter, a brochure, a response card, and a compelling envelope.) This client seemed like he wanted something that would generate leads and business quickly.

Because I had done a lot of consulting with physicians and health care facilities, I knew that many of the people making changes in their practices read the "Professional Practice" classified section of Sunday's *New York Times*. This section lists offices for rent, practices for sale, partnerships, and various business opportunities for professionals in the health care industry. The people who read this section are precisely the kinds of people my client wanted to reach. More importantly, we could start advertising in this section of the paper almost immediately.

I suggested that we begin by testing three simple headlines. Each advertisement would cost approximately $150 per insertion. We could run these ads for a year for much less money than it would cost to embark on a direct mail campaign. Besides, it is very difficult to reach doctors with direct mail because their secretaries often screen their mail, which is usually cluttered with an abundance of sales messages. My client liked the idea of using the classified section. He was also pleased because he could look forward to some instant feedback shortly after the advertisements ran in the paper. Sometimes, time is of the essence in the advertising business, particularly when your client is working in an industry hit hard by a recession.

After writing a few dozen headlines, my client and I came up with four that we decided to test: "Expanding Your Practice?"; "Is Your Waiting Room Full?"; "Imagine A Park Avenue Office At An Affordable Price"; and "My Son's A Doctor. And You Should See His Office." We also had to come up with a name that would communicate the idea that this company specialized, and had expertise, in medical construction. After generating a list of twenty-five names, we decided to use Medical Arts Construction. This seemed to communicate exactly what we wanted to in three words.

The body copy in each advertisement explained that the company was fully licensed and insured and had more than twenty-five years of experience. We also mentioned that the company offered free estimates. Our claims were supported by the fact that we had a list of physicians who were very satisfied with the projects the company had been done for them. Upon request, my client could furnish people who responded to his ads with references written by satisfied physicians.

My client received calls the very first week the advertisement ran. This is always a good sign. It usually means that the copy is on track, that the medium is a viable one, and that there is a sufficient interest and demand for the service or product being offered. If you get no responses at all, even after this kind of advertisement runs once, it may mean that there is something wrong with the whole advertising plan. We rotated each headline for about four months and we kept careful data on the number of calls, the quality of the leads, the size of the jobs, the number of jobs bid on, and the number of appointments each headline produced. The ads generated a substantial amount of feedback for my client and unlike his competitors who were sitting on their hands, my client was out there making contacts and strengthening his presence in the medical construction field. Moreover, after testing the advertisements, we found out which headlines pulled the best. Given this information, we rolled a display campaign that we ran in local medical trade journals (Figures 13 and 14).

As you will note, I also created a logo to enhance my client's image and make the advertisements more appealing. Like the classified advertisements, these ads were successful in generating leads, contacts, and business for this company. Furthermore, they positioned this business to grow once the recession came to an end. This case illustrates how classified advertisements can be used to build a business and how these same messages can be used to test headlines and copy for larger and more costly display ads. This kind of testing can be quite informative, helpful, and valuable for a wide range of entrepreneurs and small business owners.

There are a lot of different variables you can test in print and electronic media. Below is a list of some of the variables that should be tested. Most of these factors can be evaluated by running a split-run test in which you vary one item but run the ad in the same publication or medium.

1. You may find it useful to test long copy vs. short copy.
2. You may test a neat and orderly layout against a busy one.
3. You can test one headline against another. In some cases, changing just one word can make a huge difference in your response rate.
4. You can test color vs. black-and-white. Sometimes, color is not worth the additional production and media costs; sometimes it is.
5. If you are utilizing direct mail, you may want to determine if paper of one color outpulls another. You may also want to compare the pulling power of a short letter with a longer one, or an envelope with advertising copy vs. one with no copy.
6. It's also easy to test one medium against another, regardless of the form your advertising takes. You can also test various radio stations, publications, and mailing lists.

FIGURE 13 and 14. These two advertisements communicate the idea that patients will be taken care of right away.

93

In summary, careful testing is a very valuable tool for the entrepreneur who is growing a company and who wants to use his or her advertising dollars in an intelligent and pragmatic manner. Once you find out what works, you can allocate your advertising budget with a great deal of confidence.

Chapter 7

The Adventures
of a Mail Order Entrepreneur:
Direct Response Advertising

I have done a lot of testing of advertisements and commercials while running my advertising and publishing businesses. How I got started in these ventures is a bit of a long story, but I believe it is worth telling, since a lot of you can learn much from my successes and failures.

As you read through this manual, you are probably getting the feeling that I am a bit of a jack-of-all-trades. Well, for better or worse, I guess this is true. For many years, I erroneously believed that I had to do just one thing in my life. After all, that's what most people in my family did. They were either lawyers, judges, psychologists, teachers, university professors, or business people. I learned over time, however, that doing just one thing is often boring and that many entrepreneurs, like myself, run several ventures at one time because they tend to be high-energy people with lots of ideas. Many entrepreneurs, in fact, run businesses in several different fields. One entrepreneur I know oversees dozens of varied businesses in several different fields.

Fortunately, I have now found a balance in my life and enjoy the variety, stimulation, and different kinds of challenges and experiences I am exposed to when I wear each of my several hats. While I was wearing my shrink's hat a number of years ago, I was struck with what I thought was a very interesting and exciting idea. I was practicing in Las Vegas, Nevada, at the time. Las Vegas is a very interesting place, and I had a lot of fascinating therapy clients when I worked in that city. I counseled people from all over the world who had migrated to Las Vegas because it was a boom town in the late 1970s, while much of the country was in a recession. My clients also included many people who worked in the entertainment industry: actors, comedians, singers, dancers, models, showgirls, circus performers, and choreographers.

The client who was the inspiration for this new product worked in the entertainment industry. No, she wasn't a singer or a dancer or an actor. Her job was to help the showgirls in Las Vegas change their costumes during their performances. She had come to see me because she wanted to lose weight and was having difficulty staying on any kind of diet and exercise regime. I had developed an expertise in this kind of counseling, and she thought I might be able to help her. During one of our meetings, she remarked, "If only I could look like one of those showgirls. I'd give anything to be tall and slender like they are."

When she left my office, I started thinking about what she had said. I thought that there were probably a lot of other women who fantasized about looking like a Las Vegas showgirl. I had a number of showgirls as therapy patients, and many of them were quite concerned about maintaining their weight because they could lose their jobs if they gained five or ten pounds. However, the idea for what was to be my first self-help book came to me as a result of what this short, overweight, and very likeable woman shared with me during her counseling session.

To make what is already a long story shorter, I got the idea for *The Las Vegas Showgirl's Diet Book.* The title sounded very catchy, and diet books were very hot items back then. From my clinical experiences, I had learned a lot about the regimes that models, showgirls, and dancers followed in order to stay in shape. In addition, while working with these entertainers, I developed a number of motivational counseling techniques that I thought others could benefit from. In addition, I believed the showgirls could act as inspiring role models for some people who wanted to lose unwanted pounds and inches.

I asked a number of women what they thought of my idea for the book and many responded quite positively, with a great deal of interest, enthusiasm, and curiosity. I got a physician to act as a consultant and I started working on the book. I began by developing a brochure that was sold in a number of the hotel gift shops and souvenir stores in Las Vegas. This brochure was a kind of test product for the book.

I was amazed that people would pay five dollars for what amounted to a simple brochure with a diet card in it. I guess the pictures of the showgirls and the possibility (or fantasy of) looking like one of them was quite powerful. Interestingly, some men bought the brochures for their wives and girlfriends. I think that while they thought this was a useful and rather unique souvenir, they too were attracted by the showgirls' sex appeal. The brochures were selling reasonably well in the stores, so I felt that people in other parts of the country might be interested in *The Las Vegas Showgirl's Diet Book.*

At this point, I started reading everything I could get my hands on about direct mail advertising and direct marketing. From a psychological standpoint, I was totally fascinated with the idea of writing an advertisement and moving people to respond to the words and copy by sending dollars in the mail. I guess this is every mail order entrepreneur's dream. Who knows? Maybe it had something to do with my own childhood experiences with mail order, which I told you about at the start of this book.

I wrote and placed a few small classified advertisements in several tabloids, and I immediately started to get orders for the brochure. In fact, I got checks from all over the country for this simple diet plan. At times, getting these checks felt a little bit like winning the lottery. A lot of people get into mail order thinking they will just sit back, wait for the checks to roll in, and retire early to the French Riviera or Rio de Janeiro. I would be lying if I did not say that I started to have these kinds of fantasies when the checks started coming in. However, after spending a number of years in the direct response world, I learned that while a few people probably do hit it big with a particular product or offer, for most people the mail order business involves a lot of hard work, testing, and ingenuity.

There are dozens of books on how to get rich in mail order. However, for every person who succeeds in this industry, there are hundreds who fall flat on their faces. In hindsight, my success with my initial advertisements for the diet plan was possibly part luck and part skill. Many knowledgeable direct marketers plan on losing money during their initial testing phase. Fortunately, I got a fair amount of positive feedback from the initial campaign. Not only did I get a lot of orders, but the local press in Las Vegas did a few stories about me and the diet plan. I also appeared on several television and radio talk shows. Since the idea seemed to be catching on, I thought I should go ahead and write a book utilizing the showgirl theme. While I had made some money marketing the brochure, I didn't have the wherewithal to publish a book on my own. I knew nothing about printing or publishing, and I believed that most authors sought out an experienced publisher when they had an idea for a book. So I began my search for a company to publish my book.

While living in Las Vegas, I met a man who had a friend in the publishing business in Los Angeles. He explained that he had become a millionaire by selling books and products through direct response. My contact suggested that I write this fellow and tell him about my idea. I got this man's address and sent him a note along with a copy of the brochure. I didn't know that I was writing to a mail order and copywriting legend. The man's name was Joe Karbo. His famous ad for his book *The Lazy Man's Way To Riches* (1973) is referred to in just about every good book on direct response advertising. After reviewing my materials, Joe Karbo sent me a note saying that he loved the idea and wanted to publish my book. I was only twenty-seven at the time, so I was pretty excited.

I had images of my appearance on the Phil Donahue Show. I contemplated at length what it would be like to be rich and famous. After all, I had a mail order guru who "loved my idea" and wanted to publish my book. How could I miss?

The owner of a local bookstore told me I must have sent Joe a super manuscript because he was very fussy about what he would publish. Apparently, he rejected most ideas that people ran by him. I was a young kid who was flying high. I worked feverishly to finish the book. Writing my dissertation was good training for completing this task.

While writing this book was far from a scholarly endeavor, it did take a fair amount of time and discipline. I would wake up at six every morning and write for several hours each day. I finished the manuscript in about six months and sent if off to Joe. Unfortunately, I ran into some bad luck shortly after I completed my first draft.

Shortly after I moved back to New York from Las Vegas, I learned Joe Karbo had died while appearing on a talk show. His associate sent me a copy of the news story about his death a few weeks after he passed away. He actually passed away while I was driving from Nevada to New York. I was very disappointed, to say the least. Heartbroken might be a better way to describe how I felt at the time. In the short time I knew Joe, I found him to be a very bright and warm person. Each time I spoke to him we discussed a number of different ideas for future projects. Joe was quite an entrepreneur, and I was looking forward to working with him in the future. Unfortunately, for Joe, his family, and myself, things did not work out the way we all would have liked them to.

After his death, Joe's publishing company was taken over by his family members and the book was put on hold. I knew that Joe was the genius behind this business and it didn't seem as if the people running the company now had the same level of expertise or desire to market my book. I was growing rather impatient waiting for them to do something with my manuscript. In the interim, I started to do some reading on self-publishing. After learning all I could about publishing one's own book, I decided to take this route, start my company, and market the book on my own. I'm not sure exactly when I became an entrepreneur, but this moment was a key one in my development as a businessman.

As I had done with mail order advertising, I tried to find out all I could about self-publishing. I read virtually every book I could find on the subject, and I spoke to a few people who had published their own books. I named the company Skyline Press, Inc., because I was at this time living across the river from New York, in Fort Lee, New Jersey. I chose the name because it had an optimistic and upbeat connotation and because it seemed like an appropriate name for a company that would eventually publish a number of self-help products. In addition, when you name a company, it is important to select one that can be used in various media. It is also smart to have a name that is easy to spell, easy to remember, and easy to connect with an attractive logo and slogan. Furthermore, in some cases, you want to select a name that gives people an idea of where your business is located. Skyline Press seemed to meet all of these criteria. In fact, one of my consulting ventures, a spin-off of Skyline Press, Inc., is called the Skyline Consultation Group.

As it turns out, the name worked out quite well, and I did produce and market a number of successful videos, audio tapes, and books. In the course of producing and marketing these materials, I learned a great deal about package design, printing, and typography. I would ask the artists and printers I hired countless questions about what they were going to do and why. I also picked up a lot of knowledge about selecting media, testing copy, and testing different publications.

I made several per-inquiry deals with publishers that allowed me to get full pages of advertising in exchange for a percentage of my sales. Entrepreneurs who have products they want to sell through direct response advertising can still make these kinds of deals with publishers, television stations, and radio stations. However, don't bother asking the sales representative or the account executive, as they are sometimes called. Speak to the director of advertising or the owner. If they like your product and your offer, they may make a deal with you. This is a great way to underwrite your advertising costs.

While I was building my publishing venture, I attended lots of advertising workshops and seminars. I also read everything I could get my hands on about this very exciting business. I followed up the diet book with a fitness video called–you guessed it–*The Las Vegas Showgirl's Fitness Video.* I marketed the book and video through several channels, and even managed to get the tape into local video stores. A British publisher bought the United Kingdom rights to this and another book and published them in a different version under a different title in Great Britain. I also wrote a modified version of the original book that became a manual for patients in a weight control program.

I made a fair amount of money with my first step into the self-publishing industry. But what was more important was the knowledge I acquired about advertising and public relations. I conducted lots of careful tests of various advertisements, magazines, offers, and copy. I experimented with various headlines, prices, and offers. At times, I marketed the book alone; at other times, I marketed the book and the video. I had a lot of fun with these projects because I was able to watch an idea become a product. I believe this is one of the real joys of being an entrepreneur. You have an idea, which is based on a perceived need or a problem that needs solving. You then get your idea for a product into a working form, and over time, you see if you can make it fly or not. It's a real adventure. Sometimes it works out, and sometimes it doesn't. But it is always challenging and interesting. And you learn something from every success and failure.

After acquiring this knowledge, I was fortunate enough to win an advertising award from The Ad Club Of New York. This was a big thrill for me because I was competing against other people who had worked in the industry for many years. I was essentially self-taught. In fact, I was offered several jobs in large New York advertising agencies. While some of these offers were tempting, I turned them down for several reasons. First, in a large agency, they tend to pigeonhole their employees. You become either a copywriter, an account executive, a media person, or a research person. I was having too much fun running the whole show. If I had joined an agency, it probably would have been as a copywriter. As the head of one agency told me, "Jay, you could probably be a very good copywriter, but you would get bored. You would feel like you were chained to a typewriter in a corner of the agency." He felt I was quite entrepreneurial, and he encouraged me to continue to build my own ventures.

This viewpoint was echoed by several other people in the "ad biz." While at times I was a bit envious of my friends who had more traditional, conventional, and secure positions, I had a lot of freedom and I was my own boss. I made my own hours and had a lifestyle with a lot of flexibility. Sure, there is much risk, frustration, and failure that goes along with building a business from scratch. But there is also a tremendous amount of satisfaction when you create something and see it grow. Being an entrepreneur gives me a tremendous feeling of ownership, pride, and accomplishment.

As I increased my knowledge of the communications business and honed my marketing skills, I realized that I had developed some areas of expertise that could be valuable and helpful to a number of people in different industries. I had done some advertisements for several people I knew. For example, I created a brochure and some print advertisements for a clinic where I had been a psychological consultant. This project came about during a staff meeting in which the doctors were trying to find a way to get more patients. They had tried a few advertisements that fell flat on their faces, because the physicians simply didn't know what they were doing. The doctors' initial messages were boring, dull, and too technical for the patient population they were targeting. The doctors made the mistake that a lot of people make when they produce their own advertising: they wrote the message from their own viewpoint, not from their customer's. They forgot that very few people have the level of education physicians have and that most people simply lack the vocabulary and technical knowledge to read and understand an advertisement that sounds as if it were a research article written for *The New England Journal of Medicine*. (See Figure 15.)

Doctors aren't the only ones who make these kinds of mistakes. Some of the college students in my advertising courses have difficulty in writing ads for products they have no interest in. That's why I always insist that they write copy for items they would not use because this is a helpful way for these young marketers to get an appreciation for their audience's viewpoint. Young people can be somewhat self-absorbed and a bit self-centered. It is often difficult for them to view things from another person's perspective. Yet, this is a vital skill for anyone in advertising, marketing, or business to develop.

I believe my background in psychology and psychotherapy has helped me to understand things from other people's viewpoints. After all, people would frequently talk to me about a problem that objectively seemed easily resolvable and quite simple. However, during the initial phases of their counseling, it was often very complicated to them and they were, in many instances, quite upset about their dilemma or problem. As their therapist, it was important for me to understand what the problem meant to them. I needed to know why they were so upset and what fears, fantasies, and feelings the problem stirred up in their minds and their hearts. Once the clients and I had this knowledge and insight, I could help them to solve their problem, to grow, function more effectively, change, and feel better.

This same kind of knowledge was incredibly useful when I have been asked to solve advertising problems. As I noted earlier in this

FIGURE 15. This advertisement appeared in the television section of the newspaper and ran for more than a year. Notice the serious, factual copy and the play on words.

Overweight?
Now You Can Reduce In Three Spots.

Four thousand people have lost more than a quarter of a million pounds at our **three convenient locations:** Newark, Paramus and Roseland.

Since 1975, our staff of physicians, psychologists and dietitians has been helping overweight women and men to lose weight rapidly, safely and permanently.

Our comprehensive, hospital-based program includes intensive medical supervision, individual and group counseling and an educational curriculum emphasizing nutritional information, exercise, motivation, behavior modification and long-term maintenance.

Our staff is comprised of experts in the field of weight control. Our research articles are published in professional journals. We have appeared on WCBS-TV, in The Newark Star Ledger and other local and national media.

If you join our program, you will receive an abundance of support and encouragement from our team of professionals.

You are also free to choose from a variety of food plans ranging from our well-known modified fast to delicious low-calorie meals.

If you need a program which offers rapid weight loss and permanent weight control, call (201) 926-7550 to make a reservation to attend a free one hour lecture on Saturday at 9:45 A.M.

"Four Thousand Slimmer People Can't Be Wrong"

 Metabolic & Nutrition Service
(Three Convenient Locations)

Newark: Beth Israel Medical Center, 201 Lyons Avenue, (201) 926-7550
Roseland: 204 Eagle Rock Avenue, (201) 228-2045
Paramus: 351 Evelyn Street, (201) 265-7272

chapter, because I had been around a lot of professionals and knew the marketing problems associated with medicine, psychology, law, and accounting, many of my initial clients were people working in these fields. While acting as their advertising agency and marketing consultant, I continued to build my publishing company and produced a number of video and audio programs outlining some of the advertising techniques that I had perfected for people in these fields.

My publishing company's products are primarily sold through direct mail and trade shows. They are also distributed at the various marketing seminars I am asked to conduct from time to time. I continue to use the pragmatic and scientific approaches to testing that I described in this chapter and elsewhere in this manual. In the next chapter, you will see how some of these concepts are applied to an important, but sometimes overlooked medium. Figures 16, 17, 18, 19, and 20 show more examples of the various advertisements I have used to market my own products, other people's products, and my consulting work.

FIGURE 16

WILL YOU PROFIT FROM MANAGED CARE?

How To Survive And Profit In A Managed Care Environment: *A Guide For Mental Health Professionals, Clinics, Hospitals And Drug And Alcohol Treatment Facilities*
By
Jay P. Granat, Ph,D.
&
Robin Lightman, MSW

If you want your program to grow in today's market, you have to know **how to run your business in a managed care environment.** This new video shows **you dozens of proven strategies, techniques and methods to increase your profits, expand your practice and grow your outpatient clinic or inpatient treatment facility quickly, ethically and efficiently.**

Order Today And Get 4 Free Bonuses

- A half hour phone consultation with Robin Lightman, MSW. Ms. Lightman, a psychotherapist, EAP consultant, and managed care reviewer who has written and lectured extensively on managed care.
- A half-hour practice building phone consultation with Jay P. Granat, Ph.D. Dr. Granat is a marketing expert, university professor and psychotherapist who has shown more than one thousand professionals how to expand their practices.
- A comprehensive list of managed care companies
- Handy forms and charts which will make it easy for you to work with managed care companies

To Order by Phone, Call 800-336-7435
or mail this coupon

$179.95 — 30 Day Money Back Guarantee

☑ Yes, I want to learn how to grow with managed care. Send me the video and free materials. After I get these items, I will call Ms. Lightman/Dr. Granat to take advantage of my free phone consultations.

MC/VISA Card # ______________ Exp. Date ________

Signature ______________

Name ______________

Address ______________

City ______________

State ______________ Zip ________

SKYLINE PRESS, INC. 1355 15th St., Suite 290A, Fort Lee, NJ 07024

FIGURE 18

How To Accelerate Your Law Practice When You're Stuck In Traffic.

2 New Cassettes Show Lawyers 101 Guaranteed Practice-Building Methods

You're driving to your office and your mind is on business. Your practice is doing okay.

But you want to speed up your financial growth and attract more clients. You want to expand your practice quickly and ethically.

Why waste your precious time when you're caught in traffic when you could be learning the same proven techniques that produce a 200% to 800% profit for your competitors?

How To Expand Your Law Practice With Cost Effective Advertising And Public Relations: 101 Ways To Get And Keep More Clients shows you how to increase your profits while you drive to your office.

made by lawyers who don't use the tested methods described on this two hour, two volume audio program.

You'll know how to improve your relationships with existing clients.

If you're already promoting your practice, you will get lots of ideas for improving your present campaign.

Guarantee

Follow these methods for thirty days. If you're not satisfied with the results, return the audio for a full refund.

Narrated By A Lawyer

This two hour audio cassette is narrated by Philip Bryce, Attorney At Law.

largest personal injury firms in the northeast. Here's what the head of this firm says about his marketing.

"Dr. Granat has done a super job for us. I recommend his agency to other lawyers with the utmost confidence."

According to Jules Coven, A New York attorney, *"Granat's ads have had a significant impact on my practice."*

A New Jersey negligence lawyer called him "a marketing genius."

Dr. Granat's clients have appeared on Sixty Minutes, 20/20, Good Morning America and Nightline.

A Small Investment Earns Big Profits

FIGURE 19. Here's an advertisement for a golf product. Notice the big promise in the headline.

"Add 20 Yards To Your Game In 3 Weeks Or Pay Us Nothing."

Golf's greatest legends show you 500 proven tools, gadgets, techniques and programs. Lower your score. Powerize your swing. Stay on the fairway. Pinpoint your short game. Win more bets.

NEW BOOK PLUS FREE GOLF LESSON

This 278 page book comes with a free Sway Away. Use this teaching tool at your home/office. In 30 seconds you will set up perfectly. End rocking, swaying and weak shots forever! $34.95

(21 Day Money Back Guarantee)

Skyline Press, Inc.

Box 785, Ridgefield, NJ 07657

FIGURE 20. Your business card is an important marketing tool. Do something memorable with yours. Here is the copy from my "indestructible card," which reminds people of my agency and the creative campaigns we had the capability of producing.

> # Tear This Card
> # And I'll Do Your Advertising for FREE
>
> JPG   **Jay P. Granat, Ph.D.**
> Advertising • Public Relations • Marketing
>
> 1110 River Rd., Suite 103   (201) 224-4680
> Edgewater, NJ 07020

Chapter 8

"Let Your Fingers Do the Walking": Yellow Pages Advertising

Several months ago, I gave a lecture on small business advertising to a group of small business owners who were attending a series of intensive seminars at The Entrepreneurial Center at Manhattanville College in Purchase, New York. I usually begin this kind of lecture by asking people what advertising, marketing, or public relations problem they would like me to solve for them.

Invariably, questions about the Yellow Pages arise, since many business owners rely heavily on this important advertising medium. In fact, I know of many small businesses that generate all of their new customers from "phone books."

Unlike most advertising media, the Yellow Pages is the one place many potential customers look to when they have a need to purchase a product or find a service. Realize that when someone needs a plumber or a doctor, they don't sit around and wait for a television commercial advertising one of these services to appear. Instead, they let their "fingers do the walking."

According to the Yellow Page Publishers Association, the main trade association for this form of advertising, over 75% of all U.S. consumers use the Yellow Pages in the average month. In addition, 68% of consumers said they look at the bigger ads in the Yellow Pages when they're not sure where to make their purchase. Furthermore, 65% of consumers feel that a large ad in the Yellow Pages signifies a business with an established reputation.

THE YELLOW PAGES AND THE MARKETING MIX

While the Yellow Pages are often the place people refer to when they need a product or service, they can also be easily integrated with television commercials, radio spots, newspaper advertisements, and billboards. If you are advertising in other media, you ought to consider mentioning the Yellow Pages or showing the Yellow Pages logo in your other sales messages. This technique can help to build name recognition and phone number recall among your target audiences. In addition, this kind of advertising will enable the various components of the advertising effort to work together in a synergistic and more cost-effective manner.

CREATING AN EFFECTIVE
YELLOW PAGES ADVERTISEMENT

Because your Yellow Pages ad is likely to run for a year, it is important to carefully plan, write, and design this message. Many business people make the mistake of preparing and inserting their advertisement in a haphazard fashion. This is a costly error, since many of these messages appear in more than one phone directory for an extended period of time. Unlike a newspaper advertisement where an ad can be easily updated, edited, designed, or modified, a weak Yellow Pages advertisement will be in front of potential clients and customers eyes for many months. Get the most out of your Yellow Pages campaign by carefully planning your phone directory program.

An Attractive, Compelling, and Convincing Ad

Some Yellow Pages categories are quite congested and crowded. If you want to stand out in a congested marketplace and surpass your competitors, you must develop a Yellow Pages ad that is the most attractive, compelling and convincing message in your category (see Figure 21).

To some extent, an ad in a phone directory is very much like any print message. And many of the same rules and guidelines that I noted while discussing print advertisements also apply to Yellow Pages advertisements. That is, the ad must have an attention–getting visual and headline and it must give the person compelling reasons to call your office instead of the company who advertises on the

FIGURE 21. Here is an example of an effective Yellow Pages advertisement. Note the photo and the information copy.

"In Case Of Injury, We're The Legal Team You Can Depend On."

If you've been injured, you can get free legal advice from a team of experienced attorneys.

If you, or a loved one has been hurt, you may deserve a large cash award.

After a free, confidential interview, we will tell you how to protect your legal rights!

If we accept your case, we'll stand by you from beginning to end.

If you've been hurt in a car accident, on the job, by an unsafe product or by a doctor's mistake, you owe it to yourself to contact one of the largest and oldest personal injury law firms in New Jersey.

There are never any legal fees unless we collect money for you. There may be costs in some cases which are payable at the conclusion.

Our sixteen attorneys, para-legals, research staff and secretaries provide courteous, professional and efficient services at our four convenient locations.

We'll even provide free transportation to our offices.

Shevick • Ravich
Koster • Tobin • Oleckna & Reitman
A Professional Corporation

Call today for your free consultation!

RAHWAY	EAST ORANGE	JERSEY CITY	ATLANTIC CITY
1143 St. George Avenue	60 Evergreen Place	921 Bergen Avenue	1 S. New York Avenue
(201) 388-5454	(201) 672-6551	(201) 653-0101	(609) 344-7158

next page. While it is not always easy to stand out in a cluttered category, there are a number of additional guidelines that can help you profit from your phone directory advertisements.

Don't Be Boring

Take a look at your competitors' ads in your local phone directory and note how many of them look the same. Many of them begin with the company name and list what they do, with bullets at the start of each phrase or item. Many of the ads are boring, cold, and unappealing. They lack any creative pizzazz.

Don't ever insert this kind of message in the Yellow Pages (or, for that matter, in any publication). Your advertisement must generate a positive image about your business. If your ad looks like every other message, consumers have no reason to choose you over the competition.

The Headline

The headline is perhaps the most important part of this advertisement. Many start-up entrepreneurs make the mistake of using their company's name as the headline in the advertisement. This may be a good idea if your company already has a well-known name or if that name communicates the nature of your service and its unique qualities. In fact, if you are planning on starting a business that will rely on the Yellow Pages for leads and sales, you may want to select a name that instantly communicates what you do and what makes you special. (Some entrepreneurs, in fact, select a name that begins with the letter "a" so they can get one of the first listings in the phone directory.) Realize that some people do call the first company listed in a category.

If you have already selected or incorporated under a particular name, you can probably file a trading name certificate with your county clerk and do business under several names. (Check with your attorney.) In most counties and states, this is a very simple procedure. On the other hand, if you don't have a powerful name that communicates a great deal about your business, it is best to use a headline that is informative, provocative, or interesting. Use a headline that outlines the kinds of services your business offers or the kinds of problems you can solve for your customers. Try to build a unique selling point or a persuasive consumer benefit into the headline. If you have something unique to offer potential clients or customers, you should highlight this advantage in the headline of your Yellow Pages advertisement.

The Body Copy

As I stated in the section on copywriting, the body copy should expand on your headline and give specific benefits, information, and features about your business. In a Yellow Pages ad, the body copy often includes short phrases set off by bullets. These phrases should describe what specific advantages the business offers potential customers.

Free Information

Use the Yellow Pages to offer people free information, brochures, or newsletters that will build your in-house mailing list. Once people respond to your message, you ought to do all you can to make them a part of your communications program. Whenever people call in response to your Yellow Pages advertisement, add their name, address, and phone number to your database. This is a simple strategy that many entrepreneurs never take advantage of. Remember, you are paying for the Yellow Pages space for the whole year; you might as well derive all the benefits you can from this expenditure.

Free Samples

Many entrepreneurs can benefit by offering to give something away in their Yellow Pages advertisement. For example, if you're in the restaurant business, you may offer new customers a discount or a free entree. If you run a gourmet shop, you may give away free samples. If you run a consulting business, you might offer a free consultation.

The Slogan

The slogan or tag line is the phrase or saying that ties up the main idea of your message. If you examine consumer advertising, you know how important a good slogan can be in building your firm's name and reputation. Corporations like General Electric and AT&T spend months–or even years–developing suitable slogans. Don't use clichés like "Quality Services at Affordable Prices." Generate a phrase that summarizes what you can do (and have done) for your customers or clients.

Use the slogan or tag line to encapsulate the main idea of the ad as well as your firm's mission statement. Realize that the slogan may be the last item the person will read in your message. View it as your last chance to say something that will compel people to call you.

Photographs and Line Drawings

Many business people have placed their pictures in their Yellow Pages ads. This technique can help to personalize your advertisement and increase the readership and pulling power of your message. If you decide to use a photograph, don't use a boring head shot. Use a photo showing you in your work environment, which will instill confidence in you or your company. For instance, if you are an architect, you may want to show a picture of yourself next to one of the buildings you designed. Likewise, if you are a computer consultant, you may want to have a picture of yourself working on a PC along with one of your clients.

The Design of the Advertisement

Many Yellow Pages ads have a very flat and mundane appearance. An experienced graphic artist or advertising agency can mix typefaces or use colors, borders, lines, symbols, bullets, and boxes to highlight key components of the advertisement and make the message aesthetically appealing. Make sure your ad jumps off the page and grabs the reader's attention.

The Logo

Like the headline, copy, and design of your ad, your logo can communicate a great deal about your company. If you don't have a logo, hire a graphic artist or an experienced advertising agency to create one that can be used in your firm's brochure, letterhead, and Yellow Pages advertisement. Interestingly, some companies have made their logo the visual focal point of their Yellow Pages advertisement. If you have a strong logo and a well-known company name, you may elect to make your company's symbol the focal point of your Yellow Pages ad.

GENERAL YELLOW PAGES STRATEGIES

Once you create an effective advertisement, it is important to understand some of the effective techniques and strategies for profiting from the Yellow Pages.

Make Sure You Are in the Right Directory

During a recent seminar, a patent attorney asked me why he got a poor response to his Yellow Pages advertisement. The reason was quite simple: He should have never had his message appear in a consumer directory, since consumers rarely have need for a patent lawyer. If you don't provide services to consumers you should consider using business-to-business Yellow Pages or directories that serve the industries and trades in which you have your expertise. Make sure you are in the directory that is read by your target audience.

Local and National Yellow Pages Advertising

If yours is a business with multiple locations in various cities or states, you may want to consider a national Yellow Pages program. There are advertising agencies and consultants that specialize in this kind of advertising. If your business needs this kind of broad exposure, you ought to contact the Yellow Pages Association or work with an agency or consultant who can help you to plan this kind of campaign.

Select the Right Heading(s)

Some businesses ought to be listed under several categories. For instance, if you are in the construction business, you may also want to be included in the home renovation, real estate, roofing, or plumbing sections. You need not place the same-size ad or the same copy in each category. In fact, it may be totally inappropriate to use the same message in different sections, since consumers have different concerns when they need a roofer as opposed to when they want to remodel their kitchen.

Several Small Ads or One Large Ad?

Some Yellow Pages directories will allow you to advertise several times in the book. This is a way of getting your company name into your category several times. In addition, this strategy may make sense if your firm has several different, but related, areas of expertise. For example, a law firm may elect to place an in-column space ad under bankruptcy and place another in-column space ad under real estate. In some regions, these small ads outperform larger ads. It is interesting to note that some potential clients may feel more comfortable responding to a smaller ad because they associate a smaller message with lower fees and more personalized service.

Coupons and Special Positions

As was noted earlier, some of my clients have had success by offering free samples and discount coupons in their Yellow Pages ads. These coupons are usually referred to in their advertisements. This is an appropriate strategy for a wide range of businesses, and it may be something you want to consider for yours.

You may also want to think about placing your message on the front, back, or inside cover of the phone directory. These positions, while very costly, can be very effective. However, they are usually only effective for products and services that a wide range and larger number of consumers are likely to use.

Which Yellow Pages?

Many communities are now served by several directories. If you are unfamiliar with the various books, you may want to consult with other business owners to determine which company's book is the most effective one in your area. In some areas, people rely on the large directories published by the phone companies and large national corporations. In other areas, people seem to gravitate toward the smaller, more localized books because they want to contact someone who is close to their residence or business. In addition, it is also easier to go through these smaller and more compact local directories than it is to sort through a directory that is larger than the Old Testament.

Keep Accurate Data and Records

A good way to determine which directory is most cost-efficient for you is to simply test the same ad in both books. The only component you should change is the phone number. If you keep track of the calls you get from each book for six months or a year, you will know which book is best for you.

Don't Let the Yellow Pages Create Your Ad

I have heard too many horror stories about the Yellow Pages staff of copywriters and art directors to be able to recommend these people with any degree of confidence. Use an experienced advertising agency or consultant in order to get a superior advertisement for your firm. As I noted earlier, there are a number of agencies that specialize in Yellow Pages advertising. Check your local directory or your business-to-business Yellow Pages.

Chapter 9

Brochures That Bring in Big Bucks

Brochures, like other marketing communication tools, can serve a number of important functions for small business owners and entrepreneurs. Before writing, editing, designing, and printing any brochure, it is important to consider a number of questions, issues, and guidelines about the piece:

1. *What function do you want the brochure to perform for your company?* Brochures are used at trade shows. They are placed in waiting rooms. They are sent to people who want more information about your firm. They are used as leave-behinds after seminars. And they are integrated into sales presentations, media kits, and direct mail campaigns. Sometimes, they have a single use; other times, they have multiple uses. I have consulted with many entrepreneurs who say they want a brochure but have no sense of what they will do with it. Don't put the cart before the horse. Your brochure should fit in with your overall advertising and marketing plan. It should never be the other way around.

2. *Is your brochure something you plan to use once, or do you plan to revise it periodically?* If you plan to update frequently, you may elect to create a company newsletter. Or you may decide to use a folder-type brochure that can hold sales material, letters from satisfied customers and reprints of relevant trade articles. This under-utilized format is very versatile and it can grow as your business grows. It can also be filled with different materials and be used for a multitude of purposes.

3. *Will the brochure be used in a direct mail campaign?* If it is, you need to consider the size of the envelope it will fit into

and you also need to be aware of the weight of the piece and the postal costs you will incur with various kinds of brochures.

4. *When considering the size of the brochure, you must think about several factors.* First, as we noted earlier, while most brochures are designed to fit in standard business envelopes, there are some drawbacks to this format. For example, some people react negatively to the standard 8 1/2 × 11 two-fold because they see this format so frequently. Second, larger formats that fold in unconventional manners can produce a more powerful impact and increase the reader's involvement with the printed piece. Give some careful thought to the impact you want to make with your printed piece and choose a size that will present your company and products in a flattering manner. Don't restrict yourself to a traditional two-fold brochure.

5. *Who will be reading the brochure?* Are they people who already know about you, or are they people who are unfamiliar with your venture? As with all marketing communications, a different tone may be required depending on your audience.

6. *What is going to appear on the cover of the brochure?* Traditionally, many businesses place the company name on the cover of the brochure. In a lot of cases, there is nothing wrong with starting the brochure this way. In fact, in a lot of situations, this is the only reasonable and logical way to begin a brochure. On the other hand, it is often useful to view the cover of the brochure as being analogous to the headline of an advertisement or the first five seconds of a commercial (see Figure 22). As in these sales messages, you must grab your reader's attention and compel him or her to open the piece and scan its important elements. To a large extent, people will judge your brochure by its cover. So make it as appealing as possible.

7. *What kinds of pictures and graphics will liven up your brochure and make your story more interesting?* A brochure that is all copy tends to be quite boring and unattractive. Intermingle text with photographs, charts, and graphics.

8. *Which colors will project the image you want to portray?* Remember, colors have a wide range of psychological meanings. Choose tones that fit your industry, your office decor, your target audience, the mood or feeling you want to set for your reader, and the image you want to project and maintain for your company.

9. *The same holds true for the typeface or typefaces you choose for your brochure.* In some instances, you will want to mix and combine typefaces to highlight certain segments of the brochure. Other times, you may want to use the same typeface throughout. The typeface should also fit in with your logo and with other printed materials you have created for your company in the past.

10. *What kind of paper is most appropriate for your brochure?* There are hundreds of different paper stocks from which you can choose. You must decide whether you want a glossy stock, flat stock, or textured stock. In making this decision, you must again consider the image you want to project, the cost and availability of the paper, and the size of the brochure. Have your printer or graphic artist show you samples of different paper stock.

11. *The printing costs on brochures can vary widely.* I suggest that you get at least five quotes on every printing job of this kind. As you will discover, some printers specialize in various kinds of projects. Work with a printer who has produced the kind of brochure you want for your company. Look for a printer who has all the equipment needed to print, fold, score, staple, and bind your job in-house. Working with a printer that has these kinds of capabilities will save you time and money.

12. *The same holds true for the writers, artists, photographers, advertising agencies, and public relations agencies assisting you in developing your brochures.* Look for people who have produced the kinds of pieces you would like your company to have. Furthermore, make sure you work with people who will keep you informed of how the brochure is progressing through each stage. This will help to avoid any surprises or disappointments when the job is finished.

13. Many entrepreneurs have produced their own brochures in-house. While computer technology has made this possible for a number of firms, my own feeling is that communications professionals still seem to produce better products than do non-professionals. After all, these people are apt to have the technology as well as the training and experience required to produce a quality printed piece. You may find it valuable to rough out a brochure on your personal computer or desktop publishing system and use it as a rough draft to show your agency, artist, or marketing consultant. However, I have seen very few in-house brochures that were as good as those created by professional designers and graphic artists.

SURPRISE! YOU MAY NOT NEED
A BROCHURE

Make sure you really need a brochure before you have one created. Many businesses can use personalized letters in lieu of a brochure. If you plan on sending out information to customers, you may be able to save a lot of time and money by utilizing a personalized letter in conjunction with some printed information. In fact, in some instances, personalized direct mail letters outperform brochures. Apparently, a letter is still not immediately viewed as a sales pitch. Consequently, people sometimes pay more careful attention to it than they might to a more traditional brochure.

If you are going to use a letter instead of a brochure, here are a few guidelines you may find helpful. (Realize that there are dozens of books on this subject. I am merely trying to give you a few general rules for writing effective letters instead of going to the trouble and expense of creating a brochure.)

1. Make sure the letter is personalized.
2. Use quality paper.
3. Keep your letter conversational and friendly.
4. Use short paragraphs.
5. Try to do all you can to make sure your letter is read and not placed in the infamous circular file.
6. The envelope, the first line, and the heading need to be dynamite. Otherwise, your letter will get tossed.

7. Underline key words and phrases.
8. Use bold type when appropriate.
9. There are many books and computer programs containing letters that have already been prepared and tested. You may want to look at these model letters to get some ideas about the kind of letter you want to write.
10. Consider addressing the envelopes by hand. This has been shown to increase the likelihood that the envelope will be opened.
11. Don't believe the widely held notion that long letters outpull short letters. I have tested both and can tell you that I have seen instances where short notes outperform three- and four-page letters.
12. Always include a P.S., and always sign with a felt-tip pen. These techniques tend to improve readership because they enhance the personalized feeling of the letter.
13. Use direct mail in conjunction with telemarketing when this dual approach seems appropriate. You can use your letter to introduce your phone call, if you so desire.
14. When appropriate, be sure to include a business card, a reply card, or a Rolodex card.

FIGURE 22. This attorney used a simple two-sided flier in lieu of a brochure, which was sent to psychiatrists, psychologists, marriage counselors, divorce mediators, and pastors. These professionals gave this information piece to their clients and patients.

8 Facts You Should Know About Divorce

HOWARD J. PFEFFER
Attorney at Law
Edgewater Commons
81 Two Bridges Road, Fairfield, NJ 07006
(201) 227-9111

EIGHT FACTS YOU SHOULD KNOW ABOUT DIVORCE

1. **Consider Your Decision Carefully**
   A divorce is a serious and final act! Make sure your situation justifies this drastic remedy.

2. **Counseling**
   In some cases, marital counseling can resolve difficulties between you and your spouse. If it works, a divorce may be unnecessary.

3. **Prepare For Stress**
   Studies have shown divorce to cause extremely high levels of stress—second only to the stress caused by the death of a close family member. If necessary, you should talk to a mental health professional so you can deal more effectively with the stress.

4. **Consider Your Children**
   Try to keep your divorce between you and your spouse. Do your best to keep your children out of the conflict.

5. **Focus On Long-Term Issues**
   Issues like alimony and child support are more important than short-term problems such as how the wedding gifts are divided. Concentrate on long-term issues.

6. **If Possible, Settle Your Divorce**
   Approximately 90% of all divorces filed are settled, and not tried by a judge. It is in your best interest to work for a prompt, amicable and inexpensive settlement.

7. **Retain An Accountant**
   The new tax laws have had a big impact on divorce cases. Work closely with an accountant to be sure that your divorce settlement maximizes your own interest.

8. **How To Choose An Attorney**
   Pick a person who will work to resolve your situation amicably. Attorney fees for contested divorces are quite substantial. A competent matrimonial attorney will minimize these costs so you can save money. Because of the extremely intimate relationship between attorneys and clients in divorces, you must have trust and confidence in your lawyer. Retain a lawyer who you personally feel comfortable with.

Chapter 10

How to Create Great
Television Campaigns
on a Small Budget

The growth of cable television and the advances in video production technology have created numerous opportunities for savvy entrepreneurs. Before talking about some of the cost-effective ways to use this powerful medium, I would like to give you a few general rules to bear in mind with regard to creating an effective commercial:

1. Realize that the first five seconds of the commercial are vital. This is the critical point where people might change channels. You might think of the start of a commercial as being analogous to the headline of a print advertisement. While some commercials do save their best for the last five seconds, in most instances, you need to lead from your conceptual strength and create something exciting or memorable right at the get-go. Think about the commercials you like and you will probably discover that you can recall the first few scenes or frames quite vividly.

2. Most effective commercials have one key visual that contains the most important, compelling, and memorable aspect of the message. In the Michelin Tire commercials, it is probably the babies in the tires. In the Honda commercial, it is the car on the museum wall. In the old Hertz commercials, it was the driver being deposited in the car seat from high above the convertible. When you think about creating a commercial for your product or service, you may want to identify the key

visual before you actually write the rest of the spot. If you have one scene or image that carries the essence of your message, you probably have created a commercial that will be easy to remember.

3. As I noted elsewhere in this book, I have taught hundreds of people how to write advertisements and commercials. Over the years, I have observed that good print advertisements are often easily transformed into an effective television commercial. If you already have a good print campaign with a rich concept, you should be able to build a story board from this advertisement. In some cases, the same holds true for radio commercials. Similarly, sometimes what works in radio will also work in television.

4. If you don't know where to start when you begin to create your television commercial, think about a way of transforming your business or product into the hero of the spot. Think of your product as being The Lone Ranger or Superman and write the copy for your commercial from this perspective.

5. Television is a visual medium, but it also involves sound and words. Consequently, you can begin your spot with an unusual or attention-getting visual image, sound, tune, word, or phrase.

6. Effective television commercials successfully integrate sight, sound, and motion. Give careful thought to the way the visuals, the dialogue, the sound effects, and the music will all work together. In some instances, you may elect to use a soundtrack that contrasts with the visuals you are showing in your spot. This kind of unusual linkage is part of what makes television a magical medium. Use these magical powers to present unusual, attention-getting images that do not exist in the minds of your target audience. Special effects, extreme close-ups, and unusual camera angles can help to make your spot more appealing and more memorable.

7. Think about the pace of the spot. Many commercials are produced in what might be described as an MTV format. A quick pace with lots of cuts and different scenes is very exciting and appropriate for some products, but a slower pace may be right for another. For example, you probably wouldn't

use a lot of quick cuts if you were creating a commercial for a plastic surgery group. But this might be a very exciting and acceptable format for a fast-food restaurant.

8. Try to create a commercial that will entertain people, inform them, and persuade them to do whatever it is you want them to do.

9. Produce a commercial that is easy to like, easy to understand, and easy to remember. Many outstanding commercials are very simple.

10. A commercial is a thirty- or sixty-second story, adventure, tale, or show. Think about how you can use these precious and costly seconds most effectively.

11. As with messages you have created for other media, try to develop a campaign theme that you can stay with, adapt, expand on, or utilize effectively for many years. You can get a lot of mileage and utility out of a rich idea, as opposed to a concept that has only short-term appeal. The Maytag Man, Danny, The Honda Salesman, and Charlie The Tuna have been around for quite some time. Each of these characters has produced a lot of recognition, brand awareness, and profits for their respective companies and products. In your own advertising, try to create a character, theme, or story that will stand the test of time.

12. When you can, try to incorporate some of the hypnotic techniques I outlined earlier into your television spots. For example, do something in the first five seconds that will pique viewers' curiosity, causing them to wonder what is going on and what will happen next. As I noted elsewhere, a lot of advertisements and commercials are interesting and effective because they produce this feeling in the viewing audience. The Federal Express spots in which the man is speaking very rapidly and the Krazy Glue spots in which the man is hanging from his construction helmet are just a few examples of commercials that capture the viewer's interest long enough for them to watch the spot. In addition, both of these commercials have some entertainment value, so people enjoy watching them repeatedly.

WRITING AND PRODUCING
TELEVISION COMMERCIALS

I cannot possibly teach you how to become a television producer in this book. However, I can give you a few pieces of advice about writing and producing effective spots that should point you in the right direction.

First, as you probably know, virtually all ideas for commercials are written as story boards long before they are produced. Boards, as they are called, are incredibly valuable tools. They give you a sense of the timing, continuity, transition, content, and pace of the commercial. They also give you an idea of: the number of cuts; the words that will fit with each spot; the camera angle; the type of shot (close-up, medium, etc.); the position of the actor; the location of the product; the appropriate lighting; the points at which music is used; when voice-overs start and when they stop; the complexity of the editing; and the general overall effectiveness of the idea.

Those of you inexperienced with television production may never have realized all of the factors and elements that must be considered in order to create an effective commercial. As I mentioned above, even if you are a novice when it comes to producing television commercials, the story board can help you determine if your spot is going to be an effective one. If your story board is well organized, smooth-flowing, and based on the sound advertising principles mentioned throughout this manual, you are probably headed in the right direction. Conversely, what sometimes seems like a good idea simply doesn't work when you try to transform it to story-board form. Similarly, once you get your commercial into a story-board format, you may realize that creating the spot the way you envisioned it will cause you to exceed your production budget. Use your story board wisely. If you spend your time and energy intelligently at this stage, you will avoid making a lot of costly mistakes when you actually produce your commercials.

FINDING THE RIGHT PRODUCTION COMPANY

At some point in the creation of your television commercial, you will need to hire a production crew. Finding the right people to produce your spot can be almost as tough as finding the right advertising agency. (See Chapter 14.) The development of inexpensive but good-quality video equipment has caused the television industry to become saturated with thousands of production companies. A person with a video camera and a few lights can now start up a production company in his or her basement or garage. On the other hand, there are many high-end production companies with state-of-the-art, high-tech equipment that may not be necessary for your purposes. Here are some guidelines you ought to consider before you select your production company.

1. You will be spending a lot of time with the people producing your commercial. Lighting, shooting, and editing a television commercial can get pretty stressful at times. Equipment can break down, the weather can be uncooperative, and actors can make mistakes. In addition, the more people involved in the production of the spot, the more complicated things are apt to get. Make sure the chemistry between you and your production company is right, because you will be working with these people until your commercial runs on the air. Disagreements over creative decisions and technical matters can turn the production of your message into an aggravating nightmare.

2. If it seems like you can have a decent relationship with the members of the production company, you ought to show them your story board and see what kinds of thoughts, ideas, and creative input they come up with when they see the nature of your commercial. If you like what they have to say, you should ask to see samples of other commercials they have created. If these commercials resemble the type of message you want for your company, you may have found a team you can work with effectively.

3. Some of you may have your advertising agency choose your production company. Many advertising agencies select production houses in a somewhat different manner than you probably would. That is, in most instances, agencies have a cadre of directors and production companies they rely on for various kinds of productions. They usually try to match a particular kind of director and producer with a particular kind of spot.

For example, some directors and producers specialize in commercials that look like documentaries, while others like to shoot spots resembling MTV videos. As I explained, it is important to have a production team who can create the kind of message you envision for your venture. Some agencies choose directors on the basis of politics and friendships. As I noted earlier, one of the best ways to tell if you have a good match is to see the demo reels of the production companies you are considering. If you like, you can also begin your search for a production company by calling a number of producers, directors, and camerapeople and ask them to send you a copy of their demo reels.

BUDGETING GUIDELINES FOR TELEVISION

While it is important for you to set a comfortable budget no matter which medium you plan to use, it is particularly vital for you to develop a suitable budget when you consider producing a television commercial. In brief, if you don't know what you need and what you are buying, you can get ripped off badly on your television production costs. In developing your television budget, you should keep in mind the following recommendations.

Producing the Commercial

Commercials are shot in a variety of formats: Betacam; one inch; three-quarter inch; super VHS; high-speed Betacam; and film are among the formats widely used by production companies today. Each format has some advantages and disadvantages. Depending on the nature of your commercial and the size of your budget, you will need to select a suitable format.

Video technology changes rapidly, and what I write today may be obsolete or inappropriate in a few months. Nevertheless, a lot of entrepreneurs can produce an outstanding commercial by using an experienced Betacam crew. While this format does not give you the same elegant and rich look that film generates, both Betacam and high-speed Betacam are quite versatile and they can provide you with outstanding results at a relatively reasonable price. While any production professional can easily differentiate a commercial that has been shot in film as opposed to video, many laypeople cannot distinguish Betacam from film. Again, this is not to say that film is not appropriate in some instances. However, it is interesting to note that a client of mine who was ready to spend $60,000 on a commercial to be shot in film was quite pleased when I was able to write and produce two thirty-second spots for under $20,000.

Look at commercials that have been shot in a variety of formats and see which suit your needs. Work with a producer, director, lighting expert, and camera operator who have an abundance of experience in whichever format you select. An experienced crew should be able to show you the advantages and disadvantages of using various formats, equipment, and kinds of cameras.

Talent

If you are going to use actors, announcers, and musicians, you must make sure you hire the right personnel. In many instances, you can get excellent talent at an affordable price if you use people who are not members of the various acting unions and guilds. You can use non-union talent if your spot is going to run on local or cable stations. If you are going to run on network television, you may need to check on whether the station will air spots with non-union personnel.

If you need an actor, place a small advertisement in *Backstage*, the trade publication of the entertainment industry, and describe the kind of person you are looking for. In all likelihood, you will be swamped with dozens of résumés and head shots in a few days. The intense competition among actors will make it easy for you to find the right person. Several years ago, I placed a one-inch advertisement in *Backstage* for news anchorman/anchorwoman types. I received well over two hundred résumés in two weeks. You can also contact modeling agencies or talent agents and see if they have some appropriate people for you in their files. Although this might be a bit more costly, because the agency gets a commission, it may speed up your search. If you are working with an advertising agency, they usually have a personnel file of talent they have used in the past.

Whether you search for talent on your own or work with an agency, make sure you pick people who project the kind of image you want for your business. Also, be sure to use people who have appeared in commercials before. Some good stage actors simply don't have the right skills for working in front of a camera. You don't want someone to freeze up when the cameras start rolling, since this will cost you a lot of time and money. (Some actors have demo tapes that will give you a good idea of how well they manage on-camera situations.)

By the way, actors can often give you a lot of good ideas on the content of your spots, suitable camera angles, gestures, and expressions. In addition, they may have a suggestion as to how a part of the commercial ought to be produced. Listen carefully to their suggestions. They have been very helpful to me, offering dozens of good ideas.

Whether you hire a union person or a non-union person, make sure you have the appropriate release form and contracts. I suggest that you consult with an experienced entertainment lawyer before you produce your commercial. There are a lot of legal matters you must be aware of when you begin to use television; an experienced attorney can help you stay on top of these issues.

Shooting Days and Editing Days

Two more factors affecting the cost of producing your commercial are the number of days it will take to film or tape the spot and the number of days or hours it will take to edit your message. In most instances, it takes much longer to edit a commercial than it does to film it. Many production houses have day and half-day rates for shooting, and many editing houses have hourly rates for the use of their facilities and editors. Find out what the current editing rates are and try to shoot the commercial in a manner that will simplify the editing process.

You can also minimize some of your costs if you write sixty-second commercials from which you can "lift" a thirty-second spot. In many instances, you can build shorter spots by using tape from the longer commercial. Whenever possible, write your spots in a manner that will enable you to use some shots more than once.

Number of Cameras

Another factor influencing the cost of a commercial is the number of cameras you will be utilizing. The more cameras you use, the more lighting people you need, the more sound equipment you use, and the more personnel you will require. Realize that many fine commercials are shot with one camera; if the producer and director are skilled in editing techniques they can make the spot look as if several cameras were used.

Number of Locations

As you might expect, the greater the number of locations, the more expensive your spot will be to shoot. If you can limit the number of times the crew needs to set up and break down, you can help to control your costs.

Special Effects

There is no end to the kinds of special effects you can build into your commercial. Some editors and directors are special effects junkies and they love to incorporate dozens of digital effects, spins, flops, and graphics into whatever commercials they develop. These "bells and whistles" can get very expensive. Make sure you really need and want them before you get stuck paying for them. Also, be certain they will enhance your commercial. Some of the high-tech commercials being aired these days are rather ineffective communication devices. In short, make sure the special effects are really special—and appropriate—before you use them. If your editor or director recommends them, find out why. Often, a stylistic preference is simply not a good enough reason to incur an additional cost.

Copies of Your Commercial

Television stations have different requirements as far as the kind of tape they will accept for broadcast purposes. While making copies of your commercial is not very expensive, you should ask what your production company will charge to create copies in the format that is appropriate for the stations on which your spot will air.

What Will This Commercial Cost?

As you may have noticed, I have not discussed specific costs for television commercials in this chapter. That's because the amount varies a great deal from one segment of the country to another. In addition, when business is slow, most production companies are very eager to negotiate deals with potential clients. I have produced a number of successful commercials for entrepreneurs that were in the $10,000 to $20,000 range. You can have a very basic commercial created for a lot less. On the other hand, there is virtually no limit to how much money you can spend, depending on the complexity of the spot, the director's reputation, the nature of the special effects, and other factors mentioned above.

Shop carefully before you move into the production phase.

As I said at the start of this chapter, television can be a very powerful advertising tool for many small business owners. The following section describes a low-budget spot I produced that has had a substantial impact on one of my client's businesses.

THE LONE RANGER RIDES AGAIN

Earlier, I mentioned the idea of turning your product into the hero of the spot. I suggested that you think of your product or service as being like Superman or The Lone Ranger. Several years ago, I employed this kind of thinking in what turned out to be a very successful, but relatively inexpensive, advertising campaign. The campaign came about after I was contacted by a Chicago-based attorney named Terry Hepp. He had heard about my consulting work with other law firms, and he wanted me to help him with his advertising program. Terry had done some preliminary media and marketing research, and he was interested in utilizing television and radio commercials in order to expand his practice.

As I got to know this attorney, I realized that his was not a typical practice. Nor was he your typical lawyer. Terry grew up in the United States, but had spent some years in Ecuador doing charitable work for The Catholic Relief Fund. Over time, Terry developed a real affinity for Spanish-speaking people and decided that this was the population he wanted to serve when he became an attorney. When he contacted me, he had already had some notability and recognition in the Mexican-American community in and around Chicago. However, he said he was not generating the kinds or volume of cases he wanted to attract. After numerous phone conversations about his practice, his advertising objectives, his business goals, and the nature of his target audience, I began to turn my attention to the writing of his television commercials.

Fortunately, Terry had a few things going for him. First, he spoke impeccable Spanish. This can be a real asset in working with people who are new to this country and speak little English. An American lawyer who understands Mexican culture as well as the ins and outs of our legal system can instill a tremendous sense of faith and trust in potential and existing clients. Second, Terry was a rather charismatic individual. He always wore a cowboy hat to his office and to court. This hat was a ready-made logo. Lawyers, judges, court clerks, and potential clients all knew him by his trademark beige cowboy hat, which was custom-made for Terry.

After getting to know Terry and developing a feeling for his personality, I decided I would like to create a series of television commercials that would include both his famous hat and the fact that he was bilingual. Terry had explained to me that he had at times referred to himself as El Abogado Bilingual ("The Bilingual Lawyer"). Since this tag line had already produced some recognition for him, I thought we ought to keep it and continue to utilize it in his new, more extensive advertising effort. In some instances, business people want to expand one aspect of their operation. In other cases, they want to build several aspects of their operation. In Terry's case, he was interested in expanding several parts of his practice at once. Specifically, he wanted to get more immigration business, more personal injury cases, more criminal work, and more family law cases.

Since it would be hard to create a single commercial that would effectively promote all of these areas of his practice, I felt we ought to create three thirty-second spots that targeted different kinds of cases but that shared the same general theme. The first spot began with a picture of Terry, dressed in cowboy garb, riding a huge horse toward the camera. There was some traditional western music playing in the background as this beautiful horse galloped toward the camera lens. After three or four seconds, we cut to a picture of Terry standing next to the horse. Speaking Spanish, he says, "I'm not a gangster or a gunfighter." Then we cut to Terry in the courtroom, where he says, "I'm a lawyer." He goes on to assure people that he will defend them with honesty and integrity if they have been in an accident, been hurt on a job, or if they need some legal help. The commercial ends with a shot of Terry's cowboy hat on his desk. The voice-over gives his phone number and reminds viewers to remember to call The Bilingual Lawyer for a free consultation. This initial spot introduced the concept of the cowboy-lawyer. Its appeal was based on the positive associations people would make between the macho cowboy and the aggressive, hardworking, brave, and outspoken lawyer.

Another commercial featured Terry with a family that had been united in America as a result of his work on their immigration case. With the Chicago Bus Station in the background, the father states, "Now I am an American citizen and so is my whole family." He goes on to say that Terry Hepp will work hard for you and your family too. The rest of the commercial includes testimonials from other satisfied clients. A third commercial also contains several testimonials from a man who was injured on his job, a father and son who had a familial problem, and a couple whom Terry had helped with several legal matters.

All of the spots reiterate the bilingual theme. They all include Terry talking to the audience and reminding them of the fact that he will represent them with honesty and integrity. Of course, the spots also include "the hat." The television commercials were supported with radio spots that reiterated the same basic themes. This campaign was enormously successful. Terry's practice grew exponentially, and now he cannot walk down a street in the Mexican community of Chicago without being recognized. Everyone knows him as the lawyer with the cowboy hat and as The Bilingual Lawyer. The three spots were created and produced for about $15,000 and have been running for quite some time. This inexpensive effort illustrates the power of a well-conceived and well-executed television campaign.

What made this campaign so effective? I believe several factors contributed to its overwhelming success. First, I had created a novel, highly memorable, entertaining, and informative campaign. This campaign was based on a careful examination of the advertising need and on the unique and charismatic persona of Terry Hepp. Second, Terry and I went to great lengths in selecting the language we used in the spots. Terry was incredibly thorough about every word that was uttered in the commercials. He wanted to communicate the fact that people would get quality legal representation from someone they could trust. Third, unlike some clients who want to appear in their own commercials and lack the necessary skills, Terry was quite convincing and persuasive on camera. Some clients have told me they want to appear in their own commercials, and I have had to diplomatically talk them out of it. Some people just don't come across well on television. My feeling is that it is better to tell them *before* they have spent a lot of money on producing and running the spots. Furthermore, a weak spokesperson can hurt a company's image. In my mind, advertising is a little like medicine. That is, in the same way a doctor never does anything to harm a patient, I never do anything that will harm my client's business.

Terry, however, was terrific on camera. He was a bit of a ham and a bit of an actor. Like a lot of lawyers, he loved playing to a packed courtroom and he knew how to work a jury. He brought these powerful communication skills to the video camera, and they helped to make his commercials a big success. In addition, Terry's unique commercials enabled him to stand out in a legal marketplace that is now incredibly competitive. To my knowledge, no other lawyer's commercials have had the same appeal as Terry's. To some, the commercials might seem a little corny or hokey. But they had a perfect concept for his audience. Besides you can never argue with success. Moreover, I have shown these commercials at many advertising workshops for entrepreneurs and small business owners and they are always received with a lot of positive enthusiasm.

Unlike other commercials I have produced, the media selection and scheduling of these spots was a rather simple task. As you might expect, we ran them on the Hispanic television stations in Chicago. Since the spots were in Spanish, it was a relatively easy decision to make. We did, however, spend some time testing various times and frequency schedules in order to determine the best media schedule for these spots. After these tests, the commercial became a big success. For me, developing an effective message for a client is what the advertising game is all about. It is gratifying for me and rewarding for the person or persons who are building companies and paying my fees.

Chapter 11

Radio: Sounds That Sell

Like television, radio is an important medium for the entrepreneur, particularly if it is utilized in an intelligent manner. I have created a number of inexpensive, but highly profitable, radio campaigns. In this chapter, I will try to impart some of the wisdom I have derived from these experiences. Here are a few things to consider when you plan to use radio in your media mix:

1. As with television, the first five seconds of your radio spot are vital. Again, you must grab your listeners' undivided attention at this point or you will lose them. Young people in particular tend to have frenetic fingers when driving in their cars and listening to the radio, so you have got to do something spectacular right away in most instances in order to entice them to attend to your message.

2. Remember that a large percentage of your audience will probably be listening while they are driving in their cars or while they are engaged in another activity. When I evaluate a radio spot before running it on the air, I often play a cassette tape of the spot in the car to see if it works in this environment. You may also want to play your spot while engaged in another task to see how effectively it will stand out on the air. In addition, I often play the spot in the context of the programming format it is likely to run in. A spot I create for a country and western format will be very different from one airing on an all-news or all-talk station.

3. As you may recall, when creating television commercials, you want to think about the key visual for your message. When you are working on a radio spot, you need to create a

key sound that is memorable, likeable, and effectively linked with whatever it is you are selling.

4. Advertising people think of radio as the "theater of the mind," and it is useful for entrepreneurs to view this medium in the same way. Try to expand the listener's imagination through the dialogues, tempo, sound effects, and music you incorporate into your spots. Tell a story. Create a drama or mini-sitcom. Stop your listeners in their tracks. Redirect their thoughts and take them on a mind trip to a place where they would rather be. You can activate your audience's imagination with radio copy that puts them into the kind of light hypnotic trance I mentioned in an earlier chapter.

5. Capitalize on the personality of well-known radio disc jockeys and personalities by using them in your radio spots. In many markets, disc jockeys have tremendous selling power. In New York, for instance, Howard Stern's somewhat risqué format is incredibly popular, as are some of the other drive-time radio-talk-show hosts. When driving into Manhattan, I am amazed at how many people are laughing hysterically while they are stuck in bumper-to-bumper traffic. Many of these listeners are loyal followers of various radio personalities.

6. Use live reads to promote your company or product. Live reads delivered by popular radio hosts usually contain a fair amount of ad-libbing and spontaneous humor. Consequently, these spots have proven to be highly effective for many different businesses. When you want a radio personality to do a live read, you usually supply the station with an outline of the copy points you want them to cover. When they read the spot, they will frequently integrate your theme into the show's context. One of my clients was thrilled when a New York radio host spent two-and-a-half minutes delivering what was supposed to be a sixty-second spot. In addition, the announcer referred to my client by name several times during his three-hour show. The disadvantage of a live read is that the announcer may say something that is not as flattering as you would like. The wrong joke about your business may not be the best kind of publicity. However, in my experience, the

value and benefit of a live read usually far outweighs the down side.

7. Many businesses rely primarily on radio to generate customers and sales. Radio has been used effectively by automobile dealers, jewelry stores, professionals, electronics stores, municipal bond dealers, hotel chains, airlines, and resorts, to name just a few. Radio is also often used as a support medium for messages that are running in the remainder of the media mix. Think about using radio in conjunction with outdoor advertising, direct mail, print advertisements, and television. Sometimes, you can lift a soundtrack directly from a television commercial and use it in your radio campaign. In other situations, you can use radio to reinforce a jingle, slogan, or campaign theme. Some advertisers even refer to their other messages in their radio spots ("Be sure to keep an eye out for our ad in your local paper"; "Be on the lookout for your free gift in the mail"; or "We're in the Yellow Pages under . . .").

8. As I have noted elsewhere in this book, it is very important to consider the audience's state of mind when you think about using any advertising medium. This principle also holds true for radio. Realize, for example, that radio may be the first medium people are exposed to at the start of their day. Consequently, radio may be suitable for products that pertain to the morning, such as exercise equipment, coffee, and vitamins. In the same way you consider the format of the station you select, you should also consider using the kind of copy and the type of production that fit in with the time of day your spot will air. For example, a commercial airing in the morning might begin with the line "It's the start of another week, and you're anxious to get into your office as quickly as possible." A morning spot may also include some upbeat music. On the other hand, a commercial you plan to run in the evening or over the weekend may be most effective if you utilize a different kind of copy and different content. That is, you may want to use a more relaxing or laid-back message at these times in order to fit in with your audience's mood during leisure time.

9. Have your spot run adjacent to something that is relevant to your product. For example, if you are selling subscriptions to a sports magazine, air your spot close to the daily sports report or during a sports-talk call-in show. If you're selling automobile insurance or cars, run your spot close to the traffic report.

10. Take advantage of the wide range of deals radio stations frequently offer to their advertisers. Local radio stations are open to all kinds of interesting promotional activities that can be very useful for entrepreneurs. For instance, radio stations often sponsor contests, charitable events, call-in shows, and trade shows you may want to take advantage of. Entrepreneurs can usually participate in these activities by agreeing to run a certain number of spots per month. Some time ago, I did some work for a client in the real estate business. We rotated three sixty-second spots on a local real estate talk show. When the station ran a one-day real estate seminar, they put my client on a panel and gave him a booth at the exhibit hall. He handed out lots of cards and got an abundance of new business. All we had to do was commit to running our current commercials for another six weeks. Ask the radio account executives about these kinds of promotional opportunities.

11. Consider sponsoring a particular show, an event sponsored by the station, or a particular part of the programming. For instance, one of my clients wanted to reach male viewers. I suggested we run his spots close to the sports report. In addition, we had the announcer mention that the sports update was sponsored by my client's business. This proved to be a very effective use of this medium. Similarly, if a local radio station is sponsoring a bike-a-thon or a marathon, find out what kind of deal you can make to get your company's sign or banner at the event. Moreover, if you have an idea for a seminar or special event of some kind, discuss it with the managers of the local radio station. You will find that they are often quite receptive to putting this kind of program together.

12. As a rule, radio is perhaps the most negotiable of all the

advertising media. I have never paid what a radio rate card listed as the going price, and neither should you.

13. One of the big misconceptions about radio is that you always need to run a lot of spots for a long period of time in order to be effective. Many radio account executives encourage first-time advertisers to sign up for thirteen-week contracts with lots of spots running each week. While you may need this kind of frequency in certain situations, I have run some direct response commercials which have generated more calls than businesses could handle in the first two weeks of the campaign. Remember, the amount of frequency you need is a function of your advertising objectives, the number of listeners your commercial reaches, the number of radio stations in your market area, the creativity of your spot, and the strength of your offer.

SOME BIG REWARDS FROM RADIO

Effective Use of Radio Personalities

The following case example will further illustrate the manner in which a radio talk show host or personality can be used effectively. Shortly after the stock market crash of 1987, I was contacted by a law firm that wanted to represent people who were unfairly taken advantage of by stock brokerage firms. This group of attorneys wanted to help people whose brokers had placed them in unsuitable investments, who had churned their accounts to earn more commissions, or who had failed to execute transactions properly. These lawyers were initially thinking about advertising in local newspapers. I suggested live read radio spots for several reasons. One, we had several strong financial talk shows in the geographic market the attorneys were interested in reaching. Consequently, I felt that people would perceive a spot read by one of these local financial gurus as a personal endorsement of the service the lawyers were offering. Second, radio tends to be a hotter and more impulsive medium than print is. People sometimes respond more quickly to the spoken word that is calling them to action than they do to the written word. Remember, it is quite common for people to clip advertisements, put them in their wallets or pocketbooks, hang them on their refrigerator doors, and respond when they get around to it (if they do).

When someone hears a compelling radio spot with a toll-free number or an easy-to-remember local number, they often call immediately because there is nothing for them to clip and save and because they may not have a pencil handy. While I have not seen any research to support this notion, the proliferation of car phones is probably helping the direct response radio advertising business, since people can now act quickly and conveniently while they drive their cars. Another reason for selecting radio in this case was the fact that we wanted to capitalize immediately on the bad feelings that a lot of people had toward the financial markets right after the crash. I felt we could seize the moment most quickly and effectively by using radio, especially since there is no production time required when you utilize live reads.

As it turns out, this campaign was quite successful. Although the lawyers received a lot of calls from people who did not have viable cases, they did get a number of good cases in a short period of time. Furthermore, the radio campaign probably enhanced the firm's image, since the attorneys provided some valuable information and guidance to people who called their office.

I have had success with live read spots for many service businesses, and I would encourage you to consider this format if you need to get your message out in a hurry, if you want to avoid high production costs, or if you have an appropriate radio personality in the market you want to reach.

Big Results from a Few Spots

Some time ago, I developed a series of commercials for a team of industrial psychologists, university professors, and business consultants. This group offered a range of consulting services to entrepreneurs and small business owners. These announcer-read spots aired on news stations in the New York area shortly before or after the business and financial report. It cost us about $150 to run each spot, and we ran approximately six spots a week for about three weeks. The account executive from the station believed we had to test the spots for three months to determine whether this was an effective medium for this consulting group. I disagreed and insisted that we would know within two weeks whether or not radio would work out for us. As it turns out, I was right. The consulting group got thirty calls the first week the spots aired. This indicated that we had effective messages and that we had chosen the right medium. I knew that this group would continue to get more leads as the spots continued to air.

In general, if you are running a commercial with the hope of getting some immediate direct response–as opposed to a campaign intended to build brand or name recognition over an extended period of time–and you get no phone calls after the kind of short test I have described above, something is probably wrong with your message, your medium, or your business idea. In some cases, it may be more a function of the market conditions than a reflection of your marketing communications program. Perhaps there is too much competition. Maybe the economy is simply too unstable for your venture to succeed. As I explained in an earlier chapter, advertising is only one factor in the successful business equation. If used intelligently, however, radio can be a powerful communications tool for many small business owners.

Be Careful–You Can Waste a Lot of Money on Those Airwaves

Unfortunately, I have seen many entrepreneurs and small business owners make some very costly mistakes where radio is concerned. A woman with a decorating business in New Jersey was talked into spending several thousands of dollars a month on a radio station that had a rather weak signal and very poor coverage in the communities most of her clientele lived in. An aggressive salesman led her to believe that being on radio would enhance her image to the point that people would travel from New York and Connecticut for her services. However, her target audience was rather upscale, while her commercials were running on a station that targeted lower income people. What's more, the content and tone of her spots gave the listener no compelling reason to recall the name of her business or to utilize her services.

It seems this businesswoman was sold a bill of goods by the account executive from the radio station. She made some of the classic mistakes entrepreneurs make when it comes to using radio. The woman called me because she was rather distraught and upset over the money she was spending on an ineffective radio campaign. After reviewing her situation, I suggested that she get out of radio completely. Because of the nature of her business and her limited budget, I felt she should concentrate her efforts in local newspapers and an ongoing direct mail program to new homeowners in her area. Furthermore, she did have a large in-house list that she had never taken advantage of. I suggested that she start to mail special invitations to people on her customer list at least three or four times a year. As you can see, radio was probably not the right choice for this businesswoman. However, it may be right for you if you use it wisely.

Chapter 12

Where and When Should You Run Your Message?

In the last few chapters, I have described some of my own experiences and some effective ways to use a range of advertising media. In the end, the media or medium you select will be based on the answers you generate to a number of crucial questions. In this chapter, I will help you identify many of the key issues you must consider before you run your message in any medium. There are hundreds of books on media selection as well as a large number of computer programs, research companies, and databases that can help you to simplify many of your media problems. My colleague at Fairleigh Dickinson University, Dr. Don Jugenheimer, is co-author of *Advertising Media Sourcebook*, an excellent book that outlines many of the key sources of media information (Barban, Jugenheimer, and Turk, 1989). In addition, you may find it useful to work with a media buying company or a media consultant who can help you determine the best places to run your messages, select the appropriate schedule for your media campaign, and help you get the best deals available from the various media you ultimately decide to utilize in your campaign.

I frequently consult with media buyers at large advertising agencies, because they have access to a lot of useful demographic data, audience data, and computer technology that can speed up and simplify the media planning and buying process. The basic rule you ought to keep in mind is a concept that I have indirectly referred to several times in this book. I call it the "Golden Rule of Media Selection": Reach as many people who can, and will, utilize your products or service with the right message at the right time, and with the right frequency.

As has been discussed earlier, it is sometimes a little tricky for you to determine who your best potential customer might be. Similarly, what constitutes the right message and the appropriate frequency are often an issue of extensive debate even among experienced advertising experts. Realize that this is a general formula and that there are a lot of subtleties involved in media selection. Nevertheless, there are several questions and issues you must consider and evaluate before you spend any money on running your sales message.

WHAT ARE YOUR ADVERTISING
AND MARKETING OBJECTIVES?

If you have big objectives like wanting to be the number one company in a crowded and competitive industry, you will probably have to spend a lot of money on media time and space. Likewise, if you want to generate a very large number of sales throughout the country and around the world, you will need a lot of financial clout to fund your media expenditures. In short, the amount of money you will need to allocate on the media you choose is directly related to how ambitious your business goals are.

Some entrepreneurs I have consulted with tend to have rather grandiose goals and expectations for their company's expansion. However, they often come back down to earth when they discover the costs involved in obtaining extensive media coverage and in substantially increasing their market share.

HOW MUCH COMPETITION IS THERE
IN YOUR BUSINESS?

A friend of mine recently invented a food product that he hopes to distribute in major supermarkets around the country. (He has asked that I not divulge the name of his invention at this time.) The product is quite tasty, and it has a very catchy and easy-to-remember name. However, similar products made it to the supermarket shelves several months before my buddy was able to get his product into the stores.

My friend had hoped to be the first guy on the block to market his food product. Unfortunately, he has been beaten to the punch by some larger and more established companies. They have already entered the marketplace with an extensive advertising campaign and a vigorous sales promotion effort. To make matters worse, my friend lacks the financial backing to compete with widespread media efforts. In my view, he should modify his goals and instead target smaller specialty and gourmet shops, where he can better support this kind of distribution with a smaller and more manageable media campaign.

HOW EXTENSIVE SHOULD YOUR
MEDIA CAMPAIGN BE?

You may find it useful to think of media as being analogous to a public address system. The more people you need to reach, the more microphones, speakers, and volume you are going to need. In addition, if there are other people with their own public address systems trying to communicate with the same people you want to reach, you are going to need more and more equipment. If the auditorium gets more crowded, you will have to reach people at other times and other places.

HOW MUCH MONEY CAN YOU AFFORD
TO SPEND ON MEDIA?

A bottom-line reality that you must consider in both your message development and your media campaign is the amount of money you can afford to spend on these components of your company's communication program. One of my clients wanted to roll out a national advertising campaign for his new venture. His plan was to have Bo Jackson act as the spokesman for his firm. When he learned what it would cost to get Bo and what it cost to run the commercials he had conceptualized, he quickly lowered his sights and used–in a few smaller markets–a retired but well-respected athlete who had a substantial amount of name recognition.

While you may not be able to afford the kind of media effort you have dreamed about, it is useful for you to think about what you would do if you had unlimited funds. Engaging in this kind of hypothetical thinking can help you discover some exciting concepts and some powerful media plans. Then, as in the case above, you can come back down to earth and develop something that utilizes the same strategies in a more affordable and realistic manner.

Although there are guidelines that point out what similar businesses usually spend on advertising (in relation to sales), these guidelines are not always relevant for entrepreneurs who are functioning in new or atypical situations. While it is useful to look at what other related businesses spend on advertising, it is perhaps more sensible to think in terms of whom you need to reach and what you want to accomplish with your media campaign. Then, set your budget according to these objectives.

WHERE DO YOUR CUSTOMERS COME FROM?

The location of your business, the places where your products are available, and the location of your customers have a lot to do with your media choices. For instance, if you have a retail shop with one location in a small town, it makes little sense for you to advertise beyond a ten- or twelve-mile radius of your store. Your media choices in a case like this are quite straightforward: the local newspaper, the local Yellow Pages, direct mail, local television, radio, and maybe some billboards around town. It is easy for the owner of this kind of business to make reasonable media choices.

On the other hand, if you have a national company with many locations, your media plan becomes quite a bit more complicated, since media strengths vary from region to region. For example, magazine readership tends to be stronger in the Northeast than in the South and Southwest. Some people believe that this difference is attributed to regional differences in the literacy rate, the way people spend their leisure time in various sections of the country, the different ethnic groups that reside in various parts of the United States, and differences in commuting styles. That is, people in the

Northeast rely on mass transit to get to and from work. People in the South and Southwest tend to drive. Consequently, they tend not to read magazines while commuting.

As you can see, media decisions can be quite complex. Sometimes, I select media by first eliminating what seems most inappropriate for a client and then focusing on what appears to be the most viable option or options. This approach seems to help me get to the right decisions quickly. These alternatives are selected by adhering to a number of criteria, which I will discuss below.

HOW COMPLEX IS YOUR MESSAGE?

Take a walk in any shopping mall, supermarket, or shopping district and you will see all kinds of very simple and direct messages: "One Day Sale!" "Buy Three And Get One Free!" "50% Off On All Coats Today!" These messages are so straightforward that they require very little time and very little explanation. People get the idea instantly and they are able to easily respond to the message and take action if they so desire.

However, when you need to reach people with a message that requires more involvement than reading a sign, you are probably going to have to scream a little louder and a little longer to get your point across. If your message is somewhat complex, or if there is a subtle difference between your venture and a lot of other ventures, you will probably need more time, space, and frequency to hammer home your point.

WHEN ARE PEOPLE GOING TO BE MOST INTERESTED IN YOUR MESSAGE ?

Another factor to consider is the usage patterns associated with your product or service. In most industries, there are seasons or cycles when usage fluctuates. As a general rule, you want to spend most of your money during the times of the year when people are going to make a decision to buy. Advertising is a powerful tool, but it is pretty tough to "sell ice in the winter." So spend your advertising dollars at times when it will have the most meaning, the most timeliness, and, in turn, the most impact on your audience.

You must also think about the time of day and the state of mind of the audience you want to reach. For instance, if you are advertising a resort, you may elect to run your message in the travel section of the Sunday paper. After all, that is where people look for vacation ideas. And it seems like a logical enough decision. However, you could also make a case for running your advertisement in the business section, where people might welcome the idea of an advertisement that gets them thinking about something besides work and where your message can avoid the competition from all the other resorts and travel agents. As noted in the chapter on testing, you can test a coded coupon or different 800 number in both the business section and the travel section and keep accurate records of inquiries or responses and determine which medium produces the best results.

MATCH YOUR MESSAGE TO THE MEDIUM

Some advertising concepts are so rich and compelling that they work well in each and every medium. If you are conceptualizing a campaign from ground zero, you may want to strive for the kind of message that is adaptable to magazine, radio, television, and newspaper advertising. A message with this kind of versatility will enable you to get a lot of mileage out of your creative ideas.

However, many good advertising ideas simply do not work in all the media, and it is important for you to recognize that what works in print may not work in radio (and vice versa). Likewise, a great television concept may simply be too complex for a newspaper advertisement. Still, you need not worry if your message is suitable for only one medium. Many successful businesses have been built through the proper utilization of one advertising vehicle.

CREATIVE ADVERTISING MEDIA

When you mention the word "media," most advertising people think of newspapers, magazines, radio, and television. However, new places for advertising messages are constantly being discovered by some of the more creative advertising entrepreneurs. Some people believe that so-called non-traditional media will play an increasingly important role in the near future. Chris Whittle, of Whittle Communications, has set up television advertising campaigns in several non-traditional environments. Mr. Whittle has established a television network within many of the nation's schools. This medium allows advertisers to reach students while they are in the educational environment. Commercials air around news programs supplied by Whittle's company. Whittle has also made it possible for pharmaceutical companies to air television commercials in doctor's waiting rooms.

While there has been a fair amount of controversy about the ethics and appropriateness of advertising programs of this kind, reaching customers in the right state of mind–away from the clutter and congestion–is an important concern for the entrepreneurs of the 1990s. It is likely that advertising will continue to expand and that more and more companies will place parts of their media budgets in non-traditional vehicles like the ones described above. My own feeling is that computer information systems like Prodigy will continue to attract an increasing number of advertising dollars during the next decade.

Successful entrepreneurs need to always be on the lookout for newer and more innovative communications vehicles. Remember that you can now even advertise on condom wrappers and on the condom itself if you so desire. While this may seem like a wild and inappropriate tactic for many products, it is probably a super idea for others. In short, don't limit your media plan solely to traditional vehicles. If you do, you could be missing some big opportunities for getting your message to your audience.

INNOVATIVE MEDIA DEALS

Good businesspeople need to be aware of creative ways to save and make money when they purchase media time or space. There are a number of deals entrepreneurs should look into when selecting an advertising vehicle. For example, if you are selling a product through some form of direct response advertising, you can ask the advertising representative about working out a per inquiry (or PI) deal similar to the ones I mentioned in the chapter on my experiences with direct response marketing.

Per inquiry arrangements allow the company that owns the advertising medium to share in the profits of your sales in exchange for advertising time or space. Sometimes, the media company will also even assist you in the production of your message. For example, a media buying company was willing to produce a commercial for one of my mail order products in exchange for a piece of the action. I have worked out a few deals like this, and it can be terrific for all parties concerned. It often allows the start-up entrepreneur to purchase advertising that he or she may not have been able to afford under other circumstances. In addition, it allows the entrepreneur to test the effectiveness of various media without spending additional money on media time or space. Furthermore, once you have done a few successful per inquiry deals, it is easier to replicate this kind of arrangement with other publications and stations.

There is a down side to per inquiry deals, however: the media often want about forty percent of your gross sales. See what kind of deal you can work out and decide whether you can still turn a profit if you plan on advertising on a per inquiry basis. If you cannot make a profit, you must then determine if the testing and visibility you will obtain will still be worthwhile. Realize that some advertising is run with the intention of generating information for the business owner. When I place mail-order advertisements for one of my own products, I often expect to lose money during the testing phase. However, once I know which message and which publications work effectively, I can forge ahead with greater confidence and with larger sums of money.

SYNDICATED ADVERTISEMENTS AND COMMERCIALS

If you're working with a small budget, you can save a lot of money by using syndicated advertisements or commercials. These already-prepared messages are available in many industries. In some instances, they have already been tested in a number of market areas. You generally lease syndicated ads and are granted permission to run them in a given market area for a specified amount of time. This prevents a local competitor from running the same message.

The disadvantage of a syndicated campaign is that it may not communicate what is unique about your operation. Companies offering syndicated print advertisements and commercials usually advertise in trade journals. In addition, if you see an advertisement you like running in another market area, you can offer to purchase the rights to run it from the company using the message or from the advertising agency that created it and place the message in your geographic location.

Likewise, many manufacturers produce commercial footage and advertising slicks for print ads that can be adapted for use in your advertising program. If you sell or distribute products made by a large company, they will usually be glad to supply you with artwork and videotape that you can integrate with your own materials. These kinds of cooperative arrangements are used routinely by local car dealers, car stereo shops, hardware stores, appliance stores, and a number of other industries.

OTHER KINDS OF COOPERATIVE
ADVERTISING PROGRAMS

Some entrepreneurs have offset their advertising costs by sharing the expenses with people who run similar businesses in nearby communities. It is quite common to see these kinds of messages being run by automobile dealers, liquor stores, and vendors who are members of the same Chamber of Commerce, professional association, or trade association.

Similarly, your suppliers will often subsidize all or part of your advertising if you feature their products in your messages. Many retailers defray their Yellow Pages advertising costs by including the logos of nationally advertised brands in their advertisements. The same holds true for newspaper advertising. Speak to the salespeople or vendors you deal with about subsidizing your advertising.

HOW TO GET GOOD MILEAGE
OUT OF YOUR PRINT ADVERTISEMENTS

If your print advertisements are well-designed, you can probably use these same layouts for a multitude of other purposes. For example, several of my clients have used the same basic layouts they used in their newspaper ads for flyers, brochures, and the Yellow Pages. Getting several uses out of advertising materials is a good way for start-up entrepreneurs to save time and money. If you can, use a format and layout that will give you a lot of flexibility.

WHAT'S THE BEST WAY TO USE
OUTDOOR AND TRANSIT ADVERTISING?

Outdoor and transit advertising can be useful media for many entrepreneurs. Several years ago, I was contacted by a young chiropractor who had just launched his practice. He had a very limited budget, but he wanted to know what was the best thing he could do to gain some quick visibility for his office. Other consultants had suggested complicated and expensive media plans that were, I believe, too expensive and inappropriate for this entrepreneur. Since he had an excellent location with a great deal of car, mass-transit, and pedestrian traffic, I suggested that he invest in an attractive and informative sign and place it on the side of his office building.

This simple strategy worked exceedingly well for several reasons. First, the chiropractor was close to a supermarket, a health spa, and a bowling alley. As you might expect, many people become aware of back and neck pain after they work out, go bowling, or carry home the groceries. In addition, the billboard provided this physician with 24-hour visibility for his advertising message. Once his practice grew, he was able to move his advertising message into local newspapers, Penny Savers, and the Yellow Pages.

Outdoor billboards and transit advertisements can produce good results for many different kinds of businesses. If you can boil your message down to a few clever words and a powerful graphic, you may be able to get some good results from this vehicle. You can also use outdoor advertising to support and strengthen your print, radio, or television advertising efforts. Large national companies do this all the time: they frequently take a key visual or slogan from another aspect of their advertising program and incorporate it into a billboard.

Transit advertising can do many of the same things for your venture that outdoor advertising can do. For instance, transit advertising can have a particularly powerful impact in cities that have subway systems and extensive bus service. Have you ever observed the way Americans behave when they are passengers on a subway? They rarely make eye contact with anyone else on the train. I suppose it is considered as inappropriate as staring at someone in a crowded elevator. On a subway or bus, however, you often have the added fear factor. In other words, people are concerned that if they are caught staring at someone, they will be physically attacked or harmed in some way.

Consequently, if people have nothing to read and no one to talk to, they will probably read the posters on the interior of a bus or subway several times during the course of an average ride. In addition, you can add a "take one" pad to your interior poster in order to provide potential customers with more information about your firm. If you like, you can support this interior campaign with signs on the exteriors of the buses or subways, or with posters in the stations and waiting areas.

Transit advertising, like outdoor advertising, is sold on the basis of how many people will notice your message in a thirty-day time period. If you like, you can buy specific routes on the mass-transit vehicles so you can target people who live in the geographic areas that seem most relevant to your business. One of the main disadvantages of transit and outdoor advertising is vandalism in urban areas. It is often very difficult to keep your advertisements in good condition, especially if they appear in inner-city areas and the transit advertising companies usually can't do much to help protect your advertising materials.

ADVERTISING SALESPEOPLE: A VALUABLE RESOURCE

While many people who sell advertising space and time are primarily interested in getting your business, some of these individuals are also incredibly knowledgeable about media buying and advertising in general. Some have worked in large agencies or for large corporations and they often know the media game inside and out. These people have taught me a lot about media selection, scheduling, and the strengths and weaknesses of various media in different market areas. Knowledgeable account executives can give you a great deal of information if you ask the right questions; so take advantage of this important resource.

Chapter 13

Publicity, Public Relations, and Advertising: A Powerful Combination

While this book is primarily about advertising, I would be remiss if I did not say a few words about public relations. Many entrepreneurs have asked me whether it is best to use advertising or public relations in order to promote their business. In many instances, I respond by saying that the answer to this question is not necessarily an either-or kind of response. While there are advantages and disadvantages to both forms of business communication, the best strategy for most entrepreneurs is to use both advertising and public relations. If you can get both of these communication forces working together, you can often accelerate your business growth.

PUBLIC RELATIONS AND ENTREPRENEURSHIP

Business owners, corporations, political candidates, institutions, and celebrities rely heavily on their image. The way the public perceives your company and your product can have a tremendous impact on your firm's growth, or lack thereof. In short, public relations counselors and agencies help to improve the way various groups feel about an organization, corporation, or individual. For the entrepreneur, a public relations campaign may be utilized to obtain positive visibility and favorable exposure for the company or venture. This publicity can take on many forms: newspaper articles, press conferences, seminars, sponsoring events, appearances on talk shows, scholarships, charitable activities, community activities, press releases, video releases, contests, fund raisers, company tours, newsletters, trade shows, brochures, guest appearances, or lectures. While this is not a complete list of all the public relations tools and techniques, it gives you some idea of the range of activities you might consider utilizing in order to enhance your company's image.

HOW MUCH PUBLIC RELATIONS DO YOU NEED?

In general, larger companies tend to have more public relations concerns than do smaller firms. Many successful entrepreneurs find that they have to devote a fair amount of their time and energy to public relations. For example, the president of a large private university who was talking to me about several problems with the school's image remarked, "I can't believe all the publics that I must be accountable to. There's the trustees, the faculty, the staff, the politicians, the students, the parents, and the neighboring community. I never realized the range of the public relations issues that were involved in running a university."

If you consider the range of publics that some companies need to maintain solid relationships with, you can understand the value and power of this communications tool. For example, a publicly held company must be concerned with the image the company has among its stockholders. That's why companies spend so much time and money preparing annual reports. Likewise, the company must be concerned with what analysts think, what the news media think, how employees feel, how potential employees perceive the company, what old and new customers believe about the corporation, what the competition knows about the business.

PUBLIC RELATIONS AND THE MEDIA

A large percentage of television and newspaper stories are the result of press releases and publicity campaigns. If you take a look at *The Wall Street Journal,* for example, you will notice how many articles are intended to keep investors and the business community informed about the range of positive happenings within publicly owned corporations. These articles help to keep investors aware of positive events that are transpiring within the company. In many instances, a positive article can have a positive impact on a company's stock price. Conversely, bad news can cause a stock to tumble.

That's why public relations practitioners often act as liaisons between the company and the media. Whenever something newsworthy happens, the public relations person or staff gets the word out–in the form of press releases–to the appropriate editors at the appropriate publications. This same information may be sent to the electronic media in the form of a video press release.

PUBLIC RELATIONS AND CREDIBILITY

As I mentioned earlier in this chapter, there are a number of well-known advantages and disadvantages to advertising and public relations. One of the main strengths of a public relations story, compared with a print advertisement, is that a news story tends to have greater credibility than does an advertisement which the public knows the corporation paid for. (There are many Americans who distrust all advertisements and commercials and who don't believe any message that a company has paid for.) Furthermore, some entrepreneurs could never afford to pay for the amount of print space or air time they might get as a result of an effective public relations campaign.

The following case example illustrates how public relations can produce the kind of visibility and exposure that many entrepreneurs dream about.

"The Oldest Baseball Bat in America"

One thing I love about my business is that every situation and problem is always a little different. Each project that comes across my desk brings with it new challenges that require careful investigation, analysis, and creativity. Plus, while you solve the problem, you get to learn about businesses and industries you never knew anything about. For instance, several years ago, I got a call from my accountant who felt I could be helpful to another client of his. He didn't tell me much, but he mentioned something about an old baseball bat. It sounded kind of interesting, so I told him to have his client call me. A few days later, I got a call from a very bright, very energetic insurance salesman by the name of Randy Burke. Randy explained that he had bought an insurance agency in upstate New York some time ago. While looking around the office one day, he came across an odd-shaped baseball bat with a small plaque on it. (The person he bought the business from explained that she and her co-workers kept the bat around in case they had to defend themselves against "prowlers.")

Randy became quite curious about this item and did some research into the origin of the bat. He found out that it was a trophy for a game played in the 1860s. He subsequently took the bat to the Baseball Hall of Fame in Cooperstown, New York. They verified that the bat was indeed one of the oldest in America. Terry originally planned on donating the bat to the Hall of Fame, so that he could take advantage of the tax write-off for which he would be eligible. However, after reviewing the financial particulars more carefully, he decided he would prefer to sell the bat. Randy told me wanted to get $100,000 for the bat. He reasoned that an effective public relations campaign might help him build the value of the item and find an appropriate buyer. Randy had already gotten some local press about the bat. The local newspaper had done a few stories on him and his trophy, and he had been featured on a local television news broadcast. However, it was clear that he needed more than local coverage if he was to find the right buyer for his treasure; he needed some national (and perhaps international) exposure.

I proceeded to develop a press kit, which included a copy of the television interview with Terry and "The Bat," along with some additional footage we added to jazz up the story a bit. Some national news organizations picked up the story, as did some larger papers across the country. I also sent the video to a number of television stations, including two Japanese broadcasting companies. Because the Japanese tend to be baseball fanatics, I felt that there might be a number of them who would like to own this unique collector's item. Sure enough, a few weeks after they got the video, one of the Japanese networks sent a crew all the way from Tokyo to Randy's upstate New York office to do a story about him and his famous bat.

Randy took the crew to the bank vault where the bat was stored. Then they shot some footage of Randy swinging the precious bat at home plate at a baseball stadium in his town. As I noted, Randy is a super salesman, and he was absolutely terrific on camera. When asked if he would sell the bat to someone from Japan, he remarked, "I would like this treasure to stay here, but this is America, and I will part with it, if the right offer is made from anyone from any place in the world." The seven-minute story aired two times on a major sports show in Tokyo. This kind of exposure was worth hundreds of thousands of dollars. Yet this particular public relations campaign cost my client only about $12,000 in consulting fees.

PUBLIC RELATIONS AND ADVERTISING WORKING TOGETHER

There are numerous examples of advertising and public relations working hand in hand to build a company's business. For instance, when a corporation produces a novel or award-winning commercial, they are likely to get a fair amount of free media exposure. This is one good reason to strive to create novel sales messages. Similarly, when a company retains a famous celebrity or well-known personality to act as its spokesperson, a press conference is often held to announce the fact that Mr. Big or Ms. Big has come onboard. Another good example of advertising and public relations working together is when a large national corporation sponsors a television program and also purchases much of the advertising time around the show. Realize that all of the college football bowl games now have corporate sponsors. Viewers see the logo on the field, and the scoreboard, as well as lots of the sponsor's commercials during the game.

PUBLIC RELATIONS IN EXCHANGE FOR ADVERTISING

While some question the ethics involved, the media's practice of giving businesses a free story in the community newspaper in exchange for an advertising contract is widespread in magazines, radio, and television. Entrepreneurs should consider taking advantage of these opportunities. An interesting article about your business can sometimes have a huge impact on your company's growth. For example, when I was doing the advertising for a hospital-based weight control clinic, we released a story about a rather interesting woman who had come to the clinic to lose more than one hundred pounds.

It seems that this lady and her husband had been trying to adopt a child for some time. However, in spite of the fact that she was a school teacher, the adoption agencies were concerned that she might literally be an "unfit" parent. They believed that her obesity would cause her to die at a young age, leaving the child with only one parent. Shortly after losing her excess weight, she was able to adopt a beautiful little child. This made for an emotionally moving story that was picked up by a number of local newspapers, national news services, and some of the national tabloids.

The woman's struggle to lose weight in order to adopt a child had tremendous human interest appeal, and it strengthened the advertising campaign that we had been running when this story came out at the same time. In fact, the clinic's phone started ringing off the hook when one tabloid picked up this heartwarming tale. Be on the lookout for stories with a high degree of human-interest. These stories can do a lot for your business, particularly if you are involved with a consumer-oriented product.

COMMUNITY ACTIVITIES

Large corporations often become involved in charitable causes and community activities because these help people to feel more positively about the company. An excellent example of this is the Ronald McDonald House, which provides hospice care for families of children with cancer. I have done consulting work with many professionals who want to build their practices. In many instances, I have encouraged them to donate some of their time and energy to community service. This kind of donation will invariably help your company in some way. Besides, you will probably get a good feeling yourself from being involved in a good cause.

I personally believe in this kind of activity, and I believe it goes a long way in terms of the promotional and networking benefits it offers to professionals and small business owners. Some time ago, when I was active in the Lion's Club, I helped them write their annual fund-raising letter. It took me a few hours, but this small investment helped me make several good contacts in the community. Most importantly, it helped to raise more money for a worthwhile cause. A lot of invaluable contacts are made at local organizations, boards, and community-based activities. Don't overlook the importance of the networking and exposure you can gain from this kind of involvement. Figure 23 shows an ad I did for AIDS awareness.

FIGURE 23. I created this public service announcement for an advertising contest in which the entry fees were donated to an AIDS organization.

ANNOUNCING THE WORLD'S FIRST DISPOSABLE LIFE SAVER.

Practice safe sex.
And save your life.

AIDS
"It's closer to home than you think."

Chapter 14

What Entrepreneurs Really Need to Know About Advertising

Whenever I consult with a client or teach an advertising seminar or workshop, certain questions and issues seem to come up over and over again. Furthermore, business people seem to make many of the same errors when it comes to planning, creating, and carrying out their advertising efforts. Although I have tried to cover many of these matters earlier on in this book, I thought I would use the last chapter to address some of the issues that have been raised in meetings with businesspeople like yourself over the years.

I hope this chapter will give you some useful advice and prevent you from making many similar mistakes.

"I'VE SPENT A LOT OF MONEY ON ADVERTISING AND I HAVEN'T SEEN ANY RESULTS"

Not surprisingly, this is one of the most common complaints clients have when they seek my help. I usually get a few calls a week from businesspeople who are disappointed, frustrated, and worried about the money they have wasted on an expensive and ineffective campaign. Typically, I approach this kind of problem in the same way a physician might diagnose a patient's ailment. I begin by trying to learn all I can about the history and nature of the business and the objectives of the advertising program. It is also important for me to get a feeling of the viability of the business at hand. Sometimes, the concept behind a business contains major flaws. I have been contacted by people who thought they had invented products, only to learn that their idea had been on the market for several years. Similarly, people have asked me to help them with "faulty" advertising when their problems really stemmed from undercapitalization, poor management, or the marketing of an inferior product.

Sometimes businesspeople look to advertising to solve problems that have nothing to do with advertising. I have, in many instances, referred people to attorneys, accountants, investment bankers, and management consultants in order to get them in touch with the right expert to solve their particular situation. If the business seems viable, and the company seems to be in reasonable financial and managerial health, I then try to get a handle on the rationale or logic behind the advertising campaign. I try to determine if it is carefully planned, logical, and well thought out. I also like to know how this troublesome campaign compares with other advertising programs in the same or related industries.

During an initial consultation, I usually ask, "What problem would you like to solve at this initial meeting?" While I can't always come up with a perfect solution after one consultation, I can usually get a general sense as to what needs to be done to get the venture moving forward. If the business idea is well researched and seems to fill a need in the marketplace, but its communication program has failed, there is probably something wrong with either the content of the message or the medium. When I analyze the message, I ask a lot of the same questions that I have discussed throughout this book. Is the message one that I can't ignore? Is there something about it that is memorable and that sets it apart from all other stimuli in the environment? Is it clear and to the point? Does the message have the hypnotic and persuasive qualities I described earlier? Does it communicate something of importance or value in an exciting manner? Is it so entertaining that people will want to hear, read, or see it over and over again? Realize that there *are* some commercials that many of us enjoy watching repeatedly. These commercials are so enjoyable that we don't mind seeing them a few times a week. While this is not an easy feat to accomplish, it is what many advertisers should strive for in their advertising efforts.

If the message content meets the general criteria mentioned above, the next issue is the media in which the message has run. As noted in the last chapter, there are a number of important issues that must be considered with regard to media selection. For instance:

Does the medium reach those we want to reach? While this question seems straightforward enough, it is more complicated than you might think. As an example, let's say you are marketing a golf product. A logical place to advertise might be one of the golf magazines. Although many of these publications have expensive advertising rates, you will probably reach a lot of golfers. But there may be some problems with this media choice. You may, in fact, be in a medium that is so overloaded with golf products that your message simply can't stand out from the crowd. Similarly, if your product is meant more for the beginning golfer than it is for the proficient and avid golfer, some golf magazines may be inappropriate for your message. In this case, you may have to consider an alternative medium, like the Sports section of local newspapers, or a general sports magazine. You simply may not be able to reach the new golfer in a high-end golf publication.

Sometimes, it is best for your message to appear in a horizontal publication. I marketed a golf product with some success by placing ads in *The Wall Street Journal*. I knew from my research that this publication had a large number of golfers among its readership. In addition, because I wanted to test the advertisement quickly, I did not want to wait three months to get into a monthly golf publication. It is incredibly easy to make the wrong choice where media selection is concerned. I was working on a campaign in which our target audience was dentists. We considered advertising in several national dental publications. However, after conducting some preliminary testing, it became quite apparent that many dentists prefer to read the state and county professional publications, as opposed to the journals with national circulation. Moreover, dentists in private practice are very different in their reading habits from dentists who work in academia or are involved in research.

Similarly, you need to be very careful when you rent a direct mail list from a broker. First, you need to make sure that the list is current. Second, in addition to considering the nature of the direct mail piece, you must decide when and where to mail your package. That is, there are some people who get so much direct mail at work that they have secretaries and assistants screen their mail for them. If you mail to busy executives, attorneys, or doctors at their place of work, your message may never get in front of their eyes. It might be wiser to mail to these people at home, where they are likely to see your piece and where they can go through their mail in a more relaxed state of mind. Moreover, some mailings fail because they are sent at the wrong time of the year. I once wasted a lot of money on a mailing to trial lawyers. I made the mistake of sending it out during the time of year when the courts were closed and when most of these courtroom attorneys were out of town.

One of the best ways to avoid an error in media selection is to carefully research your target audience and the media you are thinking about using. In addition to reading the media kit and the syndicated research reports, talk to others who have advertised in the same place. Find out if it was effective for them. If the person you talk to is not a competitor, he or she will usually speak to you in an open and honest way. And of course, remember to test and test again before you roll out your major campaign. Another all-too-common cause for an advertising failure is the way the idea is presented. I have seen instances where something as simple as moving from one-color printing to two-color printing can increase the response rate and effectiveness of an advertisement by thirty percent. Many magazines conduct readership surveys. You can learn a great deal about what your target audience likes, recalls, and responds to by paying attention to these surveys. You can find out what kind of copy is most noticed and what kinds of illustrations and graphics get the highest recall scores among the people you want to reach.

If the medium, message, and execution seem to be all right, the next issue is the number of times the message has run. Frequency, as I noted in an earlier chapter, is another very tricky issue. Many researchers have studied the idea of how many times people need to see or hear a message in order to remember the message, try another brand, or change their attitudes or behavior. While there are many general guidelines one can follow with regard to frequency, entrepreneurs in new ventures will often need to do their own testing.

I have sold thousands of books, videos, audio programs, and dozens of seminars through one-shot ads. In fact, my return rate on some of these offers does not go up when I advertise more often; it actually stays the same in many cases. In short, determining the right frequency is a very complicated process. I strongly suggest that you test the amount of frequency you need as your venture grows. Make sure you have enough frequency to get the job done, without spending unnecessary money on messages you do not really need.

HOW SHOULD I CHOOSE
AN ADVERTISING AGENCY?

Selecting the right advertising agency is an issue that frequently comes up when I talk to entrepreneurs. To a large extent, it is a lot like selecting an accountant or an attorney. That is, you want to work with an individual or company that understands your venture and that can help you to achieve your business objectives. Also, you need to work with an advertising professional or team that you have a good rapport with. Joining forces with an agency is a little like getting married. You are going to be sharing a lot of business information with your agency and you want to feel that you can trust the agency personnel and that you can get good service from them. Take a look at previous campaigns a prospective agency has produced and ask yourself if these efforts seem appropriate for your business.

Another step in the selection process is to talk to three or four entrepreneurs who have worked with the agency or agencies you are considering and find out what it has been like to work with this company. If you are dealing with a large agency, make sure you meet with the actual people who will be working on your account. Sometimes, large agencies place junior people on your business account after you sign up with them. Small accounts can be particularly vulnerable to this kind of treatment. While new advertising personnel might have some very fresh and novel ideas, you should know ahead of time whether you will be working with newcomers or veterans.

IS IT BEST TO WORK WITH AN AGENCY
THAT HAS EXPERIENCE IN MY INDUSTRY?

This is a question I am asked quite frequently, and there seem to be two sides to the answer. First, an agency that has worked in your industry (or a related industry) is most likely familiar with both the jargon and the functions of your business. Furthermore, they probably have a handle on the problems and solutions involved in running your business effectively. They may have worked for your competitors and thus have contacts that can be very valuable and helpful to you. On the other hand, such an agency may be a little stale and lack the creativity and ingenuity required to solve your communications problems in a new and exciting manner. Conversely, an agency that is new to your company or industry may bring a fresh approach to your communication problems. You will have to weigh these pros and cons and make your decision after considering all of these factors.

HOW SHOULD I COMPENSATE MY AGENCY?

Advertising agencies have traditionally been compensated for the research they perform; the advertisements, commercials, and brochures they create; and the media buying they do for clients. As you probably know, the fifteen percent media commission was once the main source of revenue for many agencies. This method of compensation has come under serious scrutiny during the last few years. Some clients believe this sum is too large in view of the fact that many of the media buys are rather straightforward and simple.

Consequently, many agencies and clients are working out other methods of compensation. Some will even base some of their fees on the performance and general effectiveness of the campaign they produce for your company. I believe that this model has some real benefits for the entrepreneur. In fact, if your agency does an outstanding job, you ought to reward them with some sort of bonus that is tied in with meeting certain advertising or sales objectives. Likewise, if their efforts fall short of these predetermined goals, the agency ought to be held accountable.

WHAT ARE SOME OF YOUR BIGGEST ADVERTISING SUCCESSES AND FAILURES?

I have told you about several of my more successful campaigns in previous chapters. Some of my efforts have produced excellent results for my own ventures and for my clients' businesses. Moreover, my agency has been fortunate enough to be selected over some fairly large advertising agencies. I have won an advertising award while I was competing against people with much more experience than myself. In addition, I have been an advertising professor at two universities, and have also been a guest lecturer at numerous institutions and organizations.

So much for blowing my own horn. I believe that all entrepreneurs should examine their business errors closely, since these mistakes are excellent learning experiences. In fact, before I started working on this book, I wanted to write a book on advertising blunders. Several editors talked me out of this idea because they felt that companies and agencies would not provide me with the necessary information. As you might expect, some executives and advertising consultants are reluctant to go public with their blunders because they are concerned that their images will be tarnished and that their careers and companies will be damaged from this kind of exposure. I suppose executives who need to be concerned with the reactions of stockholders and board members are wise to conceal their marketing faux pas.

Entrepreneurs who are building businesses, however, can learn as much by studying advertising failures as they can from examining advertising successes. If you can overlook your bruised ego, you can learn a great deal from honestly evaluating your previous mistakes. In fact, when you meet with advertising personnel for the first time, I would encourage you to ask them about their less successful campaigns. If you get no answer to this question, I would be very suspicious about working with this agency. While there are some quasi-scientific research and testing techniques in this business, it is part art and part science. Everybody–even the best people in the advertising business–makes mistakes. Here are a few of mine . . .

Several of my biggest slip-ups occurred when I started my advertising agency a number of years ago. It is quite common for clients and their agencies to disagree over the best way to proceed with a creative concept or a media campaign. However, since clients pay the bills, agencies are sometimes coerced into doing things that run contrary to what they feel and believe is appropriate. I had a client who insisted on appearing in his own television commercial. This businessman was a nice enough fellow, but he was, for the lack of a better term, a nerd. Now, some nerds can pull off acting parts in their own spots with a great deal of success. But this particular client had what I would call "anti-charisma." I tried on several occasions to kindly, diplomatically, and gently talk him out of his desire to be the next superstar of stage, screen, and television, but his ego got in the way of his business judgment. We went ahead and shot the commercial, and it was a disaster.

In retrospect, I should have said what I now tell clients who want me to do things that I don't feel are in the best interest: "I will do it your way. But I do not want to take the responsibility for bad results if this does not work out. I will, however, put myself on the line for an idea I really believe in. Let's see if we can come up with something we both feel good about–*before* we waste a lot of money." This statement usually either ends my relationship with the client or enables us to work together more effectively.

CLIENTS WHO WON'T TAKE RISKS

Some of the more conservative clients I have worked with are reluctant to take creative risks in order to have their campaign stand out in the crowd. In their minds, a new idea is acceptable when it has already worked for the competition. Then, once it appears to be a safe bet, they want to imitate this proven approach. They fail to realize that at this point it is usually too late to use the same idea or approach. The novel idea is now old news.

As I have said over and over again, if you want your message to stand out, you have got to do something novel, unique, and exciting. If you don't create something that will get people talking about what you are doing or that will motivate them to remember your company's name and products and hopefully buy the damn stuff, there is really no reason to advertise at all.

READY, SHOOT, AIM

As I explained at the start of this book, I was a rather impatient kid. For better or worse, I have grown into a sometimes impulsive adult who, in his desire to get things done, often moves too quickly. I am told this is a common behavior among entrepreneurs. My ability to work at a quick pace has worked for me and against me. It allows me to get a lot of tasks done, but I often make mistakes by forging ahead without considering the ramifications of my actions.

Several years ago, I created a few television commercials for one of my own consulting ventures. As I noted before, I have developed a number of campaigns for professionals in the health care industry. My clients have included physicians, dentists, psychiatrists, psychologists, podiatrists, clinics, chiropractors, social workers, and drug treatment facilities. I thought it would be a great idea for me to advertise my venture on some of the medical shows produced by pharmaceutical companies. I reasoned that this was a great way to reach doctors. After all, who else watches operations and lectures about various aspects of medicine except for physicians? I felt this would be a targeted medium that would allow me to reach doctors who were interested in expanding their practices. I bounced this idea off several knowledgeable advertising and marketing "experts." (some of whom have written books on business, marketing, and advertising). Several of them loved the idea. "Jay," they told me, "It sounds like you have a winner."

I produced two thirty-second spots and ran them on several local cable networks that aired the medical shows. I selected the shows that pertained most to physicians in private practice. After running approximately twenty spots a month for about three months, I gave up on this idea. While I did get several calls, I did not generate enough good leads to warrant the several thousand dollars I was spending each month on the campaign. What went wrong? As best as I can tell, very few doctors spend their leisure time watching these shows. (Interestingly, I did get calls from several nurses and from several people in non-medical fields who liked my commercials and wanted me to help them with their advertising and business development.)

In addition, my spots may not have been exciting or compelling enough to persuade physicians to call me. As I mentioned earlier, you have got to know your audience well in order to create an effective message.

My spots probably would have been more effective if they included testimonials from doctors I had done work for. Unfortunately, many local doctors do not want to share the secrets of their success with potential competitors, so this kind of commercial would have been virtually impossible for me to produce. It has also been my experience that doctors often have a difficult time asking others for help. They seem to be comfortable and secure if they remain in the role of the helper. When they become the helpee, they often get a bit insecure, uneasy, and resistant. Consequently, asking a non-medical person for assistance in building a medical practice is often a difficult thing for many physicians to do, even if they desperately need your help. In retrospect, I probably should have attacked this resistance in my commercial. It may have been a more effective strategy than the one utilized.

Another factor could have been that some doctors are still rather resistant to the idea of professional advertising. This approach may have been too aggressive, and it may have scared them off. Since I have advertised in a number of medical journals with a fair amount of success, I think the television spots overwhelmed their intended audience. Furthermore, there is still very little reliable data about cable viewership. There are estimates of course, but you can't get the same kind of information about cable viewers that you can about network viewers (through the Nielsen Ratings or other media research companies). So what's the moral of this advertising flop? Try to advertise in media that have sound data available. Also, what looks like a good idea may not turn out to be as promising as you thought it would be.

Failure is part of being an entrepreneur. I do not dwell on my business mistakes. Instead, I try to consider what I can learn from each experience. I used to always play the role of the Monday-morning quarterback. You know, second-guessing myself, saying I could have, should have, would have. After engaging in this self-defeating behavior for a while, I realized that it was counterproductive and useless. Besides, any honest and knowledgeable advertising entrepreneur makes lots of mistakes. The idea is to take them in stride and learn from them.

Another blunder that probably grew out of my "ready, shoot, aim" mentality involved a video program I direct–marketed to dentists. I had created a very successful practice development video for attorneys, and I thought I would be able to market a similar video in a similar fashion to dentists.

I wrote an advertisement that resembled the one I had used when I wanted to reach personal-injury lawyers. I reasoned, erroneously, that dentists were somewhat like attorneys, in that they were professionals who were business-oriented and would be attracted by an aggressive promise of more patients in a short period of time. While I made some money the first time the ad ran, I did not do nearly as well as I had done with the initial ads for the law video. There are perhaps several reasons for this disparity. For one, I am rather well-known in the legal community for my consulting work, but I do not have the same kind of recognition in the dental community. However, I believe my biggest error was in assuming that you can push the same buttons with dentists as you can with lawyers. That is, I thought dentists would respond to the same aggressive appeal that the lawyers had.

When the ad did not pull as well as I would have liked in the initial test, I tried to think about what may have been wrong with my approach and the appeals I chose. One day, while going to the bank, I ran into a dentist whose office is close to mine. Although he markets his practice in various manners, he is a very conservative fellow. He is very different from an aggressive personal-injury lawyer. He is somewhat shy, soft-spoken, and very low-key. Judging from him, I think I may have frightened a few dentists off with my hard-sell approach.

I have since decided to test a different kind of advertisement. An informative ad, with soft-sell style, may outpull the first ad I tested. I play golf with another dentist, and he too is somewhat low-key and reserved. He told me he walks away from any advertisement that has a lot of hype. He said he would respond more positively to a dignified approach, one that sounds very reputable and professional.

Another factor I am still uncertain about is whether I tested the most suitable journal the first time around. I ran the advertisement in a national dental journal that is supposedly read by a large number of dentists in private practice. However, I have since learned that many busy dentists read a state or local dental journal with a bit more intensity and interest. In all likelihood, a little more testing should help me to determine which approach and which journals will work best.

DON'T TARNISH YOUR COMPANY'S IMAGE

In their eagerness to expand their company, some businesspeople resort to unethical or illegal advertising tactics. Remember, you want to build your company *without* damaging your reputation. If you do something inappropriate, it could take you months or years to recover from your customers' anger and the bad publicity you are likely to receive. In addition, legal fees can be very costly these days, so it is best to play it safe. If you are in doubt about what you can do and what you can't do, get a few opinions from two or three attorneys who are knowledgeable about advertising law and ethical and unethical business practices.

LOTS OF FUNNY THINGS HAPPEN
WHEN YOU ADVERTISE

Advertising is a complex, strange, and rather amusing game. Sometimes, what you hope and pray will happen never happens. And sometimes advertising produces surprises that you would have never dreamed possible. I have seen ads that experts disliked perform quite well. I have also seen advertisements with poor graphics, cluttered designs, and mediocre copy outperform messages with beautiful layouts and typography.

Several of the businesses I have developed campaigns for have made huge sums of money in a very short period of time. Some of my clients have used the same advertisements or commercials I created for them for several years. Sometimes, they get calls from a radio commercial that ran two or three years ago. Apparently, some people jot down phone numbers, place them on the refrigerator door, and call them when the time is right. Others have had minimal success with their advertising campaigns for a multitude of reasons. Sometimes, their budget was simply too small to create the kind of impact they needed to be successful. Other entrepreneurs, who had difficulty taking input from an outside source, have simply failed to follow my advice. Some were control fanatics and could not let go or delegate any control or power. Occasionally, they were reluctant to take the kind of creative risk you have to take to get people to talk about and remember your name and your business. In other situations, the economy, an inferior product, or a highly competitive environment were simply too much for the advertising program to overcome.

As I have been saying throughout this book, there are some general guidelines that are useful to bear in mind when you plan and implement your advertising effort. However, every marketing communication problem is different. You must always be ready for disappointments, but be willing to try to find a way to make your campaign as successful as possible.

WHAT ARE SOME OF YOUR FAVORITE ADVERTISEMENTS AND COMMERCIALS?

Most advertising is mediocre. Like you, I forget or fail to notice most of the sales messages I am exposed to during the course of each day. On the other hand, I see a commercial every so often that I adore and that I can enjoy watching or listening to over and over again. The advertising campaigns I tend to gravitate toward are those that are very simple, but that somehow get me to think about things in a different way. These messages are often entertaining, amusing, clever, or informative. And, of course, they do an effective job of selling, convincing, persuading, and motivating. They push the right buttons in me and probably in others as well. They have something that makes them unforgettable.

I could probably write an entire book on my favorite spots, but I have just finished this one and I need a little time off. Here, then, are a few of my favorites, along with a brief explanation of why I like them. This is the kind of advertising you may want to strive to create for your business.

I love the Easy Spirit commercial showing the women playing basketball in high heels. This is a striking visual, and it is a brilliant way of selling the comfort these shoes offer to women. The ad's slogan, "Looks Like A Shoe, Feels Like A Sneaker," says a great deal in eight words. In addition, this message works in print as well as on television.

I also love the old Schaefer beer advertisements: "It's The One Beer To Have When You're Having More Than One." This is simply a great way to get people to consume more beer. Speaking of beer, I also like a lot of the Miller Lite commercials that used the line "Tastes Great, Less Filling." Again, these four words communicate a great deal of information to beer drinkers who are concerned about their weight.

The old M&M's commercials with the unforgettable line "Melts In Your Mouth, Not In Your Hands," along with the visual of the clean hand and the dirty hand, were brilliant. This campaign showed chocolate lovers how they could enjoy delicious candies without getting their hands messy.

The long-running McDonald's campaign that declared "You Deserve A Break Today" was terrific because everyone feels entitled to a break. After all, we all wake up with some aches, pains, complaints, or a case of the blues from time to time. Some people wake up and hope for a big break of some kind. These people may go to Las Vegas or buy a few lottery tickets in search of their break. Obviously, this was a great feeling to connect with a fast-food chain, where many busy and tired people are likely to seek sustenance.

The Kodak campaign with the "true colors" theme is a brilliant way to encourage people to take more pictures and use more Kodak film. Showing children participating in an array of events, contests, and athletic endeavors is a moving and sensible way to promote Kodak–especially since many adults with cameras spend a lot of time and energy photographing their children.

The Nike ads with Bo Jackson have it all: Great music, entertainment, the right celebrity, fantastic tempo, humor, superb editing, and a memorable tag line.

The AT&T "Reach Out And Touch Someone" campaign is right on target in the way it simply, yet effectively, evokes the reality of our increasingly "long distance" society. This is a good example of a campaign that has its finger on the pulse of its customers.

The California Raisins campaign featuring Claymation raisins is one that everybody seems to love. It is memorable, entertaining, and a great example of music and characters working together to form an entertaining, memorable, and enjoyable sales message. By the way, this commercial did significantly increase raisin consumption.

I could go on and on about all the great sales messages I have seen. But now it is time for you to create your own. Use the few I've mentioned as inspirational models. Shoot for the moon and create the greatest advertising possible. I hope that my personal anecdotes and the information included in this book will help you to create the kind of business you have always wanted. I will leave you with this inspirational message . . .

It's not the critic who counts; nor
the observer who watches from a
safe distance. Wealth is created
only by doers in the arena who are
marred with dirt, dust, blood, and
sweat. These are producers who
strike out on their own, who come
up short, time and again, who know
high highs and low lows, great
devotions, and who overextend
themselves for worthwhile causes.
Without exception, they fail more
than they succeed and appreciate
this reality even before venturing
out on their own. But when these
producers of wealth fail, they at
least fail with style and grace,
and their gut soon recognizes that
failure is only a resting place,
not a place in which to spend a
lifetime. Their places will never
be with those nameless souls who
know neither victory nor defeat,
who receive weekly paychecks
regardless of their week's
performance, who are hired hands in
labor in someone else's garden. These
doers are producers, and no matter
what their lot is at any given
moment, they'll never take a place
beside the takers, for theirs is a
unique place, alone, under the sun.

–Joe Mancuso

From the book: *How To Start, Finance, and Manage Your Own Small Business* by Joseph R. Mancuso. © 1978. Used by permission of the publisher, Prentice Hall/ a Division of Simon & Schuster.

References

Barban, Arnold M., Jugenheimer, Don J., and Turk, Peter B. *Advertising Media Sourcebook*. Lincolnwood: NTC, 1989.

Benson, Herbert. *The Relaxation Response*. New York: Morrow, 1978.

Jackson, Tom. *Guerilla Tactics in the New Job Market*. New York: Bantam, 1991.

Karbo, Joe. *The Lazy Man's Way To Riches*. Sunset Beach, CA: Karbo, 1973.

Le Cron, Leslie M. *The Complete Guide To Hypnosis*. Los Angeles: Nash, 1971.

Mancuso, Joseph. *How To Start, Finance, and Manage Your Own Small Business*. Englewood Cliffs, NJ: Prentice-Hall, 1978.

Moine, Donald J. and Lloyd, Kenneth L. *Unlimited Selling Power*. Englewood Cliffs, NJ: Prentice-Hall, 1990.

O'Hanlon, William Hudson and Hexum, Angela L. *An Uncommon Casebook: The Complete Clinical Work of Milton H. Erickson, M.D.* New York: Norton, 1990.

Packard, Vance. *The Hidden Persuaders*. New York: Van Rees, 1957.

Rosen, Sidney. *My Voice Will Go With You: The Teaching Tales of Milton H. Erickson*. New York: W. W. Norton, 1982.

Weitzenhoffer, Andre M. *General Techniques of Hypnotism*. New York: Grune & Stratton, 1957.

Yapko, M. D. *Trancework: An Introduction to the Practice of Clinical Hypnosis*. New York: Brunner/Mazel, 1990.

Yates, John M. and Wallace, Elizabeth S. *The Complete Book of Self-Hypnosis*. New York: Ivy, 1984.

SUGGESTED READING

Caples, John. *Tested Advertising Methods*. Englewood Cliffs, NJ: Prentice-Hall, 1974.

Caples, John. *How To Make Your Advertising Make Money*. Englewood Cliffs, NJ: Prentice Hall, 1983.

Lewis, Herschell G. *More Than You Ever Wanted To Know About Mail Order Advertising.* Englewood Cliffs, NJ: Prentice Hall, 1983.

Lewis, Herschell G. *How To Make Your Advertising Twice As Effective At Half The Cost.* Englewood Cliffs, NJ: Prentice Hall, 1986.

Lewis, Herschell G. *On The Art of Writing Copy.* Englewood, NJ: Prentice-Hall, 1988.

Moine, Donald J., and Herd, John H. *Modern Persuasion Strategies: The Hidden Advantage in Selling.* Englewood Cliffs, NJ: Prentice-Hall, 1984.

Ogilvy, David. *Confessions of an Advertising Man.* New York: Atheneum, 1963.

Ogilvy, David. *Ogilvy on Advertising.* New York: Crown, 1983.

Roman, Kenneth and Maas, Jane. *How to Advertise.* New York: St. Martin's, 1976.

Winters, Arthur A. and Milton, Shirley F. *The Creative Connection: Advertising Copywriting and Idea Visualization.* New York: Fairchild, 1982.

Index

A page number followed by an "f" refers to a figure.